WEAPONS
OF THE
21st CENTURY

WEAPONS
OF THE
21st CENTURY

BILL YENNE

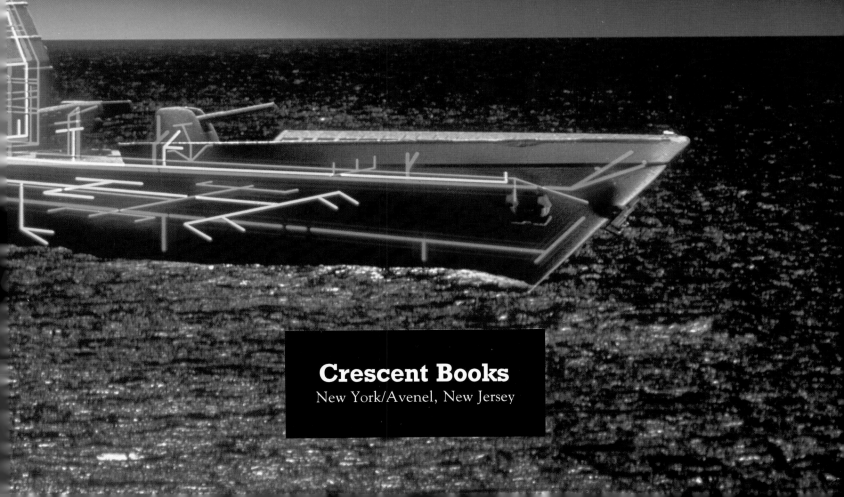

Crescent Books
New York/Avenel, New Jersey

This 1992 edition published by Crescent Books, distributed by Outlet Book Company, Inc., a Random House Company, 40 Engelhard Avenue Avenel, NJ 07001

Produced by Brompton Books Corporation 15 Sherwood Place Greenwich, CT 06830

ISBN 0-517-06976-8

8 7 6 5 4 3 2 1

Printed and bound in Hong Kong

Page 1: The X-31 experimental fighter aircraft is a joint venture between Messerschmitt-Bölkow-Blohm of Germany and Rockwell International of the United States. Its Enhanced Fighter Maneuverability (EFM) enables it to make sudden and spectacular turns.

Pages 2-3: This artist's impression depicts the vital electrical systems and circuitry of the nuclear-powered US Navy USS *Ticonderoga* class Aegis guided missile cruiser.

These pages: This illustration depicts the major air and sea components of future US Navy antisubmarine operations. **Clockwise from top left:** An SH-60B Seahawk antisubmarine/search and rescue helicopter; a P-3C Orion antisubmarine/maritime patrol aircraft; another SH-60B Seahawk; an 'enemy' submarine; a *Seawolf* class nuclear-powered attack submarine and a *Ticonderoga* class guided missile cruiser.

Photo Credits
Aerospatiale Division Systemes Strategiques et Spatiaux 43 (bottom left)
AMD-BA/Aviaplans 43 (bottom right)
Armscor 28, 28-29, 38-39, 59
AT&T 4-5
Boeing & Sikorsky 54, 54-55, 55
Bofors (Bofors Group of Swedish Ordinance) 22, 22-23, 23, 29
British Aerospace 30, 46-47
Dassault-Breguet 56-57
Katsuhiko Tokunaga Daet
Deutsche Aerospace 60-61, 62
Eurofighter Jagdflugzeug GmbH 31
GEC Avionics 7
General Dynamics Corporation 11, 12 via DOD 13 (bottom)
Israel Military Industries (IMI) 40 (both), 65, 66
Lockheed 33, 35
Los Alamos National Laboratory 52
McDonnell Douglas Corporation via DOD 74
MagneTek Defense Systems 2-3, 8-9
Messerschmitt-Bölkow-Blohm/Rockwell International 76, 76-77, 77, 78-79
Mitsubishi/General Dynamics 38
NASA 44, 45 (left), 72
Northrop via DOD 13 (top), 18-19, 20-21
Rockwell International 1, 73, 75, 78 via DOD 49 (top right)
SAAB-Scania, Olle Arpfors 47

Steyer-Daimler-Puch AG 15, 16, 17
TRW/Martin Marietta 24 (top)
United States Air Force 34, 58 via DOD 64
United States Army 42 (top), 43 (top) via DOD 42 (bottom)
United States Department of Defense (DOD) 14, 24 (bottom), 25 (all), 32, 45 (right), 49 (top left and bottom), 63 (both)
Walther Arms Works 70, 71
© Bill Yenne 10, 36-37, 50, 50-51

Designed by Bill Yenne

Edited by Lynne Piade

TABLE OF CONTENTS

INTRODUCTION:

THE TURN OF THE MILLENNIUM

by BILL YENNE

The dawn of the twenty-first century will mark the turn not only of the century but of the millennium. In the late 990s and again in the 1490s (the turn of the half millennium), prophets and doomsayers filled the literature with startling predictions. As is the case with today's annual tabloid prognostications, most of these did not come true, but the ones that took into account the evolution of trends did come true.

In the final days of the second millennium, one thing that can be predicted with certainty is uncertainty. The massive political changes in Europe and the former Soviet Union, which took place in the 1989-1992 period, altered the course of history more radically than anything else since World War II. Out of these changes emerged a new geopolitical reality. A once-divided Germany became a single entity and became the dominant economic power in Europe, as it had been a century and a half before. The once monolithic Soviet Union ceased to exist with a whimper, rather than a bang, and from it sprang a dozen new countries, some destined to become part of Europe and others destined to become part of Islamic southeast Asia.

In terms of military reality, the major focus suddenly shifted from a political conflict between NATO and the Warsaw Pact to a potential for small conflicts in previously unimagined corners of the world. The 1982-1992 period had provided a preview: the Falklands, Grenada, Panama, Yugoslavia and Persian Gulf conflicts were all military actions that could not have been predicted even a few months before they began.

After 50 years of preparation for a vast land battle on the scale of World War II, military planners—especially in the West—are now faced with having to prepare for the unknown, while at the same time responding to protests of overtaxed populations who assume that the end of the Cold War should signal an end to high defense budgets.

In this book we examine a wide spectrum of weapons, from infantry arms and surface vehicles designed for low-intensity combat, to space-based systems that were once conceived to defend against ICBMs, but which in the future may be necessary to defend against suicidal nuclear terror raids from xenophobic Third World potentates.

This book is arranged encyclopedically, but it is more of a gallery than an encyclopedia. Almost any observer will be able to cite omissions, but indeed, our intention is not to be encyclopedic, but rather to paint a general picture of the future using representative examples. This book was written in the early 1990s as a catalog of some of the weapons systems that were in service or in development at that time, and which appeared to be likely candidates for the arsenals of the twenty-first century.

Because of the expense and development time involved in modern, high-tech weapons, it is possible to make certain projections with a reasonable degree of reliability. In 1992, it was safe to say that in 2010 the Abrams, Chieftain and Leopard II main battle tanks (MBT) would be in service with the armies of the United States, the United Kingdom and Germany, but before 1989 we could not even have predicted a unified Germany.

We are safe in predicting that the F-22 Lightning will still be an important US Air Force fighter in 2015, but whether or not it would serve with any other air forces was a hard call in 1992.

Looking back at past forecasts can be amusing. The B-52 strategic bomber came on line in 1954 in an era of planned

---

Facing page: A view of a twenty-first century stealth aircraft in flight over a mountainous landscape. While this aircraft, known as Black Magic, is not representative of any actual future aircraft as planned in the 1990s, the twenty-first century will last one hundred years, so who knows? The illustration is from a series of advertisements for GEC Avionics Ltd, Airport Works, Rochester, Kent, England, and is reproduced by kind permission of GEC Avionics.

obsolescence, and was intended to be retired by the end of the 1960s, yet it was in combat in 1991 and will still be in service in 2001. The hypersonic B-70 first flew in 1964 and was expected to be the harbinger of a whole *generation* of hypersonic aircraft in the 1970s and 1980s, but it was gone and forgotten by 1974, and in 1992 there were no hypersonic aircraft in operational service anywhere.

In 1940, when the midpoint of the twentieth century was still a long and eventful decade away, the keels were laid for the first of the USS *Iowa* class of battleships. In 1946, it was predicted that the era of the battleship was over forever, and indeed, no more battleships were to be built anywhere. However, in 1991, when the United States fought its most successful war since World War II, the first salvos were fired by a pair of *Iowa* class battleships!

When 12 Apollo astronauts walked on the moon between 1969 and 1972, most people believed that by 1992 astronauts would be routinely living on the moon and others would have walked on Mars. However, *no* astronauts visited the moon between 1972 and 1992, and it seemed unlikely that any further steps would be taken on the moon during the twentieth century, and there were no plans to send anyone to Mars before 2017.

It also takes a long time to *develop* technology. This was pointed out very succinctly by American Secretary of Defense Richard Cheney when, in an August 1991 speech, he said:

'If we take that into account—the timelines that are involved in developing defense—I think it becomes obvious that we have to take a long-term perspective in developing national security policy. We cannot simply be in the business of responding to the developments of the moment.

'Teddy Roosevelt, when he was assistant secretary of the Navy back in the late nineteenth century, gave a speech once in which he complained that it took two years to build a battleship. We now have a nuclear aircraft carrier in the fleet—the USS *Roosevelt*—that was nine years in construction.

'In the [Gulf] War, over half the aircraft carriers we used were more than 20 years old. Much of the hardware that played such a crucial role in our victory over Saddam Hussein and the Iraqi forces was developed 20 and 30 years ago. The F-111 bomber that did much of the precision bombing was developed by my predecessor, Bob McNamara, and was first operational in 1967. It takes about 10 years to train a good senior noncommissioned officer in the Marine Corps and nearly a quarter of a century to train an officer capable of commanding a modern combat division in hostilities.'

Predicting technology is difficult to do, but there are certain trends that can be extrapolated. Hypersonic flight will be routine at some point in the twenty-first century, as will single-stage-to-orbit (SSTO) space flight—probably within the same class of vehicles. The 1991 Gulf War clearly demonstrated that laser-guided bombs and laser range-finders in tanks made traditional weapons more accurate

and hence more desirable. This trend will certainly continue.

When attempting to predict the nature of military technology in the twenty-first century, we should note that, at best, we only can see so far as the first two decades, an era when world battlefields will be dominated by weapons which were originally deployed in the 1985-1999 time frame.

Prophets of military technology have become more conservative of late, but it is still axiomatic to say that it always takes longer to bring a program on line than its original devotees optimistically project in its early phases. Many of these will be in service in 2025, a fair number will still be around in 2050, and it is safe to say that most will influence

Right: Advanced weapons systems require highly advanced electrical circuitry. This artist's rendering illustrates the complicated electrical network that extends throughout the body of a twenty-first century military aircraft. Such advanced technology powered the systems which operated during the 1991 Persian Gulf War.

the course of aerospace technology for much of the twenty-first century.

While there are international treaties mitigating against the presence of offensive weapons in outer space, there is no reason not to expect defensive weapons. And then there *are* treaty breakers. The twenty-first century will see the advent of the most versatile weapons ever, and it will also witness the routine use of manned, reusable spaceplanes. The United States first flew a spaceplane in 1981 and the Soviet Union followed with an unmanned test flight of their own vehicle—the *Buran*—in 1988. It was predicted at that time that the *Buran* would make a manned flight in 1989, but that prediction was repeatedly postponed. At the time the Soviet Union collapsed in 1991, it looked as if the postponement

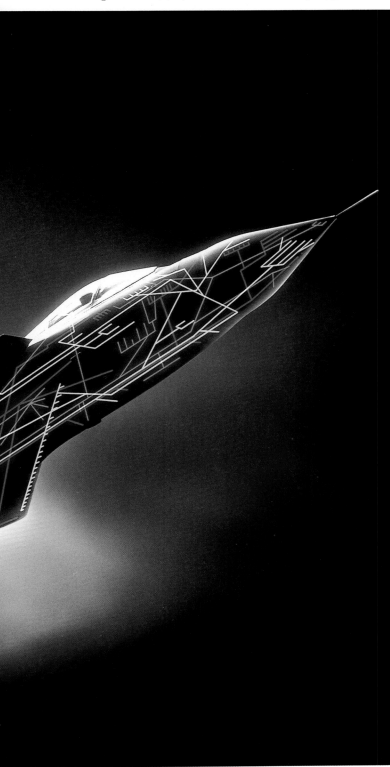

would be permanent. By the turn of the century, the Japanese are expected to have flown a spaceplane, as are the French, under the auspices of the European Space Agency. Meanwhile, both Germany and the United States are studying horizontal takeoff spacecraft. The timing laid out in the early 1990s will certainly change, but when these do first fly—in the twenty-first century—they will be the first true spaceplanes, insofar as they will not only land on runways like today's Space Shuttle, but also take off from runways.

The emphasis on aerospace technology is widely seen in the world's military community. It is particularly notable that, after the political upheaval in the Soviet Union in August 1991, the all-powerful post of Defense Minister was assumed by Marshal Yevgeny Ivanovich Shaposhinikov, who was the Commander in Chief of the Soviet air force. (Also notable here is that the Soviet air force supported Boris Yeltsin, Mikhail Gorbachev and the reformers, rather than the perpetrators of the *coup d'etat*.)

Marshal Shaposhinikov, while not a hard-liner in the mold of the Red Army men who had preceded him as defense ministers, was a thoroughly professional advocate of aerospace power. 'In the major countries of the world,' he said, 'military aviation and space technology programs have high priority.'

Indeed.

Rapid progress was made during the 1980s, both in Europe and the United States, in the development of improved avionics and land systems driven by very high speed integrated circuits (VHSIC) and operated on easily read, full-color, liquid crystal displays on control panels, as well as helmet-mounted displays.

The first aircraft designed specifically to employ the secret 'stealth' technology for avoiding radar detection were unveiled in the late 1980s, but stealth characteristics are now considered so important that virtually no future combat aircraft would be considered front-line *without* stealth technology. This technology includes both the use of new radar-absorbing materials for the structure and surface of the aircraft, as well as a whole new approach to the overall shape of the airframe. In the waning years of the twentieth century, aerospace engineers are focusing on areas of technology which would have been considered science fiction just a few years earlier, but which are absolutely essential to the warplanes of the twenty-first century. These not only include the Super Cockpit and stealth technologies, but much more. Knowledge-based systems with artificial intelligence, which use human-like logic to operate avionics and weapons, are under study. So-called 'smart skin' or 'intelligent surface' materials are being developed to replace antennas, pods and domes that protrude from aircraft surfaces and increase radar vulnerability.

Nonlinear optics will use light in radically different ways for automatic tracking or to obviate atmospheric interference. Photonics technology not only increases the capacity of computers but helps to protect them from the scourges of electronic warfare. New lubricants are being introduced, as are new propellants. Among the latter are chemical propellants of increased power and decreased weight. Forward-looking infrared sensors, that allow users to see through fog, rain and the dark of night, will become standard. Escape systems will also be faster and more reliable.

The evolution of weapons systems has gone hand in glove with the evolution of tactics. Behind the technology, of

Left: A Soviet Russian pilot waves from the cockpit of his MiG-29. This photo was taken by the author in October 1991, midway between the August 1991 Soviet coup and the December 1991 collapse of the USSR. Thus, the MiG diplomatically sports the flags of *both* the Russian Republic *and* the USSR. Two months later, the latter was removed permanently.

Facing page: Advanced military aircraft contain thousands of color-coded detail tubes which allow the circulation or expulsion of a wide variety of gases and liquids. Once formed by hand, these tubes are now fabricated by machines and cut by a highly concentrated laser beam. Specifications are input by an operator and stored on a floppy disk.

course, are the costs of its development. In the 1970s and 1980s, soaring costs prompted the emergence of international consortiums that shared both the costs and results. A good example is Panavia, the Anglo-Italian-German group that developed the Tornado fighter-bomber in the 1970s. In the twenty-first century such arrangements will be the rule rather than the exception, as the 1992 unification of European markets becomes a practical, rather than theoretical, reality. In the United States, groups of aerospace firms have already been formed to develop the ATF and ATA projects, and in Europe a multinational consortium will build the European Fighter Aircraft (EFA). Transatlantic cooperation will also become more common, following the pattern of the British Aerospace-McDonnell Douglas collaboration, which brought about the Harrier, and that of the Rockwell and Messerschmitt-Bolköw-Blohm effort that produced the X-31.

Finally, the shape of weaponry in the twenty-first century will be governed by strategic need, which will in turn be governed by the political shape of the twenty-first century world. In the period from 1872 to 1940, the strategic shape of the world revolved around a *ménage-a-trois* involving Germany, Britain and France. The United States and the Russian Empire (the Soviet Union after 1917) played important, albeit peripheral, roles.

In the period from 1945 to 1991, the most important strategic reality in the world was the Cold War between the United States with its NATO allies on one hand, and the Soviet Union with its Warsaw Pact allies on the other. Most weapons and weapons technology designed in those years were developed against the backdrop of the Cold War. In 1991, the Warsaw Pact ceased to exist. Meanwhile, the United States had ceased to be an important military and economic force in Europe, as reunified Germany became the most important power in a Europe that was more unified than ever before. Both Germany and Japan emerged as economic superpowers, their armies having achieved with

briefcases what they had failed to do with Zeros and Panzers in World War II.

If anything is certain about the military situation in the post-Cold War twenty-first century, it is the *uncertainty*. For 40 years, the major armies of the world prepared for World War II. After 1991, they were faced with preparing for the unexpected. The British prevailed in the 1982 Falklands War, but the chore was made difficult by their lack of preparation. Having retained just one of the full-sized aircraft carriers that they had earlier scrapped would have made the task of recapturing the Falklands far easier. In the 1991 Gulf War, the United States regretted the absence of the SR-71 reconnaissance aircraft that had been retired two years before.

The uncertainty was pointed up in Secretary Cheney's pivotal August 1991 speech when he asked: 'Five years from now, who will control the Soviet nuclear arsenal? Will there still be a central government in charge? Or will the Republics have taken over that responsibility? Or will the four republics that currently have strategic nuclear weapons on their soil each have its own independently controlled arsenal of nuclear weapons? Tactical nuclear weapons are much more widely dispersed than strategic systems. Will they still be controlled from the center? Or will they come under the control of the respective republic governments?'

It took not five years, but just *four months* for the USSR to crumble and for the control of the Soviet nuclear arsenal to fall into the hands of four republics. Secretary Cheney then went on to state that 'You simply do not turn around United States military capability in a matter of days or weeks. And as I look at those who made recommendations over the last 10 days that we change our defense posture, I wonder whether they want me to base our long-range strategy—that will carry us over the next 20 or 30 years—upon the status within the Soviet Union [on] 17 August, when Gorbachev was still in charge and all was peaceful; or on the situation on 20 August, when the coup plotters were in charge; or on the circumstances of 22 August, when the coup plotters had been arrested and democracy had been restored in Moscow … We simply cannot base our long-term defense needs and requirements on those kinds of momentary changes. We've got an excellent strategy in place, and we ought to stick to it over the course of the next several years.'

Because weapons follow strategy and strategy follows politics, it is hard to make predictions in a time of turmoil and rapid political change such as that which accompanied the dawn of the 1990s. With that in mind, we give you a gallery of weapons—both those of a combat and those of a deterrent nature—which will probably play roles in the conflicts of the twenty-first century.

A-12 Avenger II

System type: Carrier-borne attack aircraft
Country of origin: USA
Manufacturer: General Dynamics
Principal distinguishing feature: Triangular airframe incorporating the maximum in stealth characteristics
Status: Project terminated in 1991, but the technology forms the basis for subsequent systems

The Avenger II program—originally the ATA project—produced one of the strangest airframes, and one of the biggest planning disasters, that had ever been seen in the American defense establishment. Nevertheless, A-12 technology will probably be seen again in the twenty-first century.

In the mid-1980s, as the US Air Force was starting to define its twenty-first century fighter requirements under the ATF program, the US Navy's Naval Air Systems Command (Navair) was doing the same with its need for a new generation, all-weather attack aircraft. Like the ATF, the Advanced Tactical Aircraft would incorporate the Integrated Electronic Warfare System (INEWS) and the Integrated Navigation & Identification Avionics (ICNIA). Unlike the ATF program, however, which was widely discussed in the news media, the Navy's project was kept secret until 1986 because of its stealth nature, and even then Navair revealed as little data as it could. For example, the Navair phone directory listed Captain Sam Sayers as ATA program coordinator but didn't list his address!

In November 1986, two teams—Grumman/Northrop and General Dynamics and McDonnell Douglas—were selected to participate in the demonstration and evaluation phase of the ATA project. On 13 January 1988, the latter team was given a $4.8 billion contract to build the aircraft, which was designated A-12. In July 1988, the US Congress insisted that the Air Force and Navy cooperate on both the Air Force's ATF *and* the Navy's ATA programs in order to save money. Air Force Secretary Russell Rourke had said in March 1986 that the ATA *could* be used as an eventual replacement for the Air Force's F-111, so there was room for shared development. This could amount to 450 Navy A-12s and as many as 550 for the Air Force. The first would come as early as 1990, the last around 2008. In August 1989, the Air Force—having insisted upon 90 percent commonality between its A-12 and that of the Navy—was told that it would receive the twenty-sixth production airplane as its first.

An interesting controversy—a tiny footnote to the dreadful controversy to come—surrounding the A-12 involved the choice of a name. Most names that were proposed alluded to the stealth nature of the airplane, as it would be the first aircraft, after the F-117 and B-2, in which stealth characteristics are paramount. Included among the intriguing list of choices were Masked Avenger, Enforcer, Ghost, Mystic, Seabat, Shadow, Stingray, Veil and Avenger II.

The name Avenger constitutes an allusion to the Grumman TBF Avenger, one of the Navy's most important attack aircraft of the World War II era. It was also the plane flown by LTJG (later President of the United States) George Bush. The choice of the name Avenger was to be awkward because Grumman lost the ATA competition, and the aircraft that the A-12 would replace is the Grumman A-6. Despite this, the name Avenger II was retained.

Above: The A-12 'Flying Dorito.'

Technical problems—including weight problems—had begun to bubble to the surface in April 1990 during Defense Secretary Richard Cheney's review of the program. Navy Secretary H Lawrence Garrett III ordered a 'major reassessment.' New delays were reported in May, and the first flight, planned for October 1990, was postponed to 1992. There was also talk of a $450 million cost overrun, which grew to an estimated $852 by the end of July 1990.

In September 1990, the first pictures of the strange, triangular craft—it was called a 'flying Dorito' by those close to the project—were released, along with some details. It was 37 feet long with a 70-foot wingspan (39 feet when folded), and a wing area twice that of an F-14. It was, after all, closer to being *all* wing than any other plane in history. It was also *all* stealth. While it did have air-to-air capability, the A-12 was an attack bomber, and it had a massive internal bomb load three times that of the F-117.

The unveiling of the stealthy Avenger II should have been greeted by a high level of excitement and interest, but controversy over its cost and scheduling were deepening. On 29 November 1990, investigations revealed widespread, varying problems in the program which had not been previously reported to the Navy or the Defense Department. By December, the situation reached crisis proportions. The Navy went so far as to fire the head of Navair, Vice Admiral Richard Genz, and a week later Undersecretary of Defense for Acquisition John Betti resigned after being criticized for not realizing that the program was out of control.

On 14 December, Defense Secretary Cheney ordered the

Navy to 'show cause' why the program should not be canceled. They could not, and on 7 January 1991, Cheney canceled the A-12 program. However, the management problems should not be seen to denigrate the design. The Avenger II was dead, but the technology that it spawned would live on—in the twenty-first century.

AFA see *F-22 Lightning/F-23 Gray Ghost*

AGM-129

System type: Advanced air-launched cruise missile
Country of origin: USA
Manufacturer: General Dynamics (Convair Division) and McDonnell Douglas
Principal distinguishing feature: A stealth cruise missile with inertial guidance which has midcourse terrain update capability
Status: First deliveries in June 1990; operational status achieved in 1992

The AGM-129 was to have been the ultimate successor to the Boeing AGM-86 cruise missile that became operational in 1982. The General Dynamics design was selected in April 1983 as the basis for the system, and in 1987 McDonnell Douglas was brought in as a second source manufacturer. The 2750-pound missile, powered by a Williams F112 turbofan engine, can carry a 200-kiloton nuclear warhead 1865 miles. Equipped with conventional warheads, AGM-129s carried by B-52s were the first weapons to strike Iraq in the 1991 Gulf War. One year later, however, President George Bush announced in his 28 January 1992 State of the Union Address that the United States would 'not purchase any more advanced cruise missiles.'

AGM-136 Tacit Rainbow

System type: Air- or ground-launched, defense-suppression missile
Country of origin: USA
Manufacturer: Air Force/Navy version: Northrop (Ventura Division)
Army version: Raytheon and McDonnell Douglas

Above: The Tacit Rainbow missile has a unique pivoting wing design which permits more missiles to be carried by the launch aircraft than would be possible with a fixed-wing weapon. *Below:* The AGM-129 stealth cruise missile.

Principal distinguishing feature: Tenacious and survivable standoff of pre-launch programming, as well as weapon capable of loitering in the target area
Status: In full-scale development but future uncertain

The Tacit Rainbow project is managed by the Joint Tactical Autonomous Weapons System Program Office (JTAWSPO) for the US Air Force and US Navy. The F121 turbofan engines are being built by Williams, and Boeing is developing a rotary launcher that will permit multiple AGM-136 launches from B-52G aircraft and presumably B-1B and B-2 aircraft as well.

The jet-propelled AGM-136 was first launched from a B-52 on 30 March 1989 and from an A-6E Intruder on 31 August. It has a 40-pound fragmentation warhead. The US Navy has indicated an order for 11,762 units, and in September 1989 the US Army selected Raytheon and McDonnell Douglas to build a ground-launched version for use in its Multiple Launch Rocket System (MLRS).

An-225 Mriya

System type: Ultra heavy duty airlifter
Country of origin: Ukraine (formerly USSR)
Manufacturer: Antonov OKB
Principal distinguishing feature: World's largest aircraft
Status: Limited production after first flight in 1988, but the An-225 is likely to be the harbinger of similar, or larger, aircraft

The twenty-first century will see aircraft that are vastly larger than anything we have known in the twentieth century. The An-225 is the harbinger of truly awesome flying machines. For almost a decade the Lockheed C-5 Galaxy and the Boeing 747 jetliner were far and away the largest aircraft in service anywhere in the world. The Soviet Antonov An-124, which first flew in 1982 and entered service in 1987, was based on the Lockheed C-5. Though slightly shorter, it had a seven percent greater wingspan. However, for all practical purposes, these three airplanes were the same size. Unknown in the West until 30 November 1988, the An-124 had a big brother. When the An-225 Mriya (Dream) first flew on 21 December 1988, it did seem like a dream. The Mriya

Above: An Antonov An-225 Mriya during takeoff.

was 28 feet longer than the C-5, with a wingspan 50 feet greater than the An-124. The largest airplane ever flown, the Mriya was also the only airplane ever to have a gross weight over one million pounds.

It can be said that the An-225 is in essence a scaled-up An-124. The An-225 uses the same, albeit lengthened, fuselage and the same wings, which are extended by being moved outward on an expanded wing root structure. Whereas the An-124 was powered by four turbofan engines, the An-225 has six Lotarev D-19s, which deliver an aggregate total of 309,900 pounds of thrust, compared to 206,600 pounds available for the An-124, or 172,000 for the C-5B.

The An-225 can accommodate 16 large freight containers internally and has attachment points for carrying external cargo that can be carried in immense, streamlined containers that have a greater internal volume than most transport aircraft have in their fuselages. The An-225 is also the designated transport for the Soviet space shuttle orbiter, which it carries externally.

Mriya was used to provide heavy equipment transport services in remote regions of the Soviet Union where all-weather roads do not exist. Though flown publicly in the colors of Aeroflot, the Soviet state airline, the An-225 was an important aircraft in the service of Soviet Military Transport Aviation, as well as in its capacity to carry the Soviet *Buran* space shuttle orbiter. After the collapse of the Soviet Union in 1991, Antonov began to look beyond the former USSR for potential markets for the world's biggest airplane.

ATA see *A-12 Avenger II*

AUG A1

System type: Multipurpose assault rifle
Country of origin: Austria
Manufacturer: Steyr-Daimler-Puch AG
Principal distinguishing feature: Highly versatile and variable infantry weapon system
Status: Production

The Steyr AUG A1 (Army Universal Gun), a most modern personal weapon, is based on six main assemblies, comprising all individual parts of the various AUG versions. As a result, it is possible to produce various AUG versions, which basically differ from one another only in the length of the barrel, and cover a major part of the entire spectrum of small arms. The basic AUG versions, and the barrel lengths which distinguish them, are as follows: Commando model, 14 inches; Machine Carbine model, 16 inches; Assault Rifle model, 20 inches; and the Light Support Weapon, 24.5 inches. All main assemblies and individual parts are fully interchangeable within the AUG weapons system. In addition, there is a wide range of optional equipment, which can likewise be used with the entire AUG weapons system.

Engineered to the compact 'bullpup' design, the AUG A1 is rugged and durable, and is made to operate in a wide variety of conditions—from desert to arctic, and anywhere in between. Weapons in which the magazine is located to the rear of the trigger are said to be of 'bullpup' design. This design makes for an extremely short overall length of the weapon, about 25 percent shorter than conventional designs. The overall length with the 20-inch barrel is only 31 inches. With the 16-inch barrel, the overall length is just 27 inches. In this way it becomes possible to dispense with a folding stock version, along with all the drawbacks which that system entails. The AUG's quick-change barrel enables swift, easy fieldstripping of this firearm. Fieldstripped, its longest component measures only 21 inches. Moreover, it is instantly possible to convert the assault rifle into any one of its machine carbine, commando weapon, light machine gun or heavy barrel automatic rifle configurations.

The AUG represents the first time that an optical sight has been integrated into the carrying handle of a military weapon, and thus it is housed in a fully protected fashion. The optical sight offers a magnification of 1.5 times, providing a wide field of sight. Furthermore, it is possible to fire with both eyes open (as the human eyes are able to adapt themselves from 1 to 1.5 x). This optical sight features a standard ring reticule with a diameter of 1.8m projected on a distance of 300m. The standard ring reticule offers a further advantage by serving as an aid for range finding. Other reticules are offered optionally. An optical sight offers enormous advantages. For the average acquisition of a target via an optical sight, one reckons with 1.5 seconds (where two points must be line up), versus open sights with three seconds (where three points must be lined up). In the hours of dawn or dusk and on overcast days, the target can be made

Below: The basic AUG A1 Assault Rifle with 30-round clip.

out via an optical sight long after any hope of doing so with open sight has gone.

The AUG A1 also has an adaptable receiver for night-sighting equipment or a scope of a more powerful magnification. For all applications where optical sights cannot be used for some special reason or where their use is thought to be undesirable, Steyr also offers an AUG version with open sights. These open sights are also in accordance with all requirements of international standards and of NATO in regard to the length of the line of sight, without foregoing the advantages of the bullpup principle or any other benefits offered by the AUG weapons system.

The AUG A1 fires 5.56mm (.223 caliber) ammunition. The advantages of this small, high-velocity round are many. For example, as compared to the tried-and-true 7.62mm (.308 caliber) round, the new ammo weighs approximately half of what the 7.62mm round weighs. And, because the ammo is lighter, the weapon has a weight saving of approximately one-third.

Owing to the high muzzle velocity, the trajectory of the bullet is so flat that up to a range of 385 yards the soldier need not bother at all about the point of aim. There is no need for setting the sight. The small caliber also makes for exceptionally steady shooting; the gun will not jump, climb or swerve. Recoil is so slight as to be almost negligible. There is no flinching or fatigue. The AUG A1 features rapid changeover from single shots to sustained automatic fire and vice-versa without any need for a lever, which means that no time is wasted looking for the selector.

The generously dimensioned, cold-hammered and internally chrome-plated barrel guarantees a minimum service

Above: A cutaway view of the AUG A1.

life of 15,000 rounds, provided a maximum temperature of 400 degrees C is not exceeded (which means cooling after 150 rounds of fully automatic firing). The magazines are fracture-resistant and transparent. Thirty- and 42-round magazines are available. Cleaning is exceptionally easy, thanks to the chrome-plated barrel and the use of non-corrosive materials, such as aluminum and synthetics. No tools are needed to strip down or reassemble the weapon.

The AUG A1 has six modular assemblies. The barrel is hammer-forged of high-grade steel, and features a chrome-plated bore. In all AUG versions, the barrel is connected to the receiver lid provided on the right and on the left. The port on the side facing the shooter is closed off in each case by an ejection cover that can be used on either side. Optionally, stocks with ejection ports on the right only or left only are available.

With the exception of a small number of minor parts, the trigger assembly is also made of synthetic material. The entire trigger mechanism has been designed as a compact assembly, and, following the removal of the butt plate, can be readily withdrawn from the stock. It is controlled from the trigger via a sear lever located in the stock. The magazine consists of transparent, highly impact-resistant synthetic material. The transparent material used enables the firer to check at a glance how many rounds are still left in the magazine. Special attention has been paid to retaining interchangeability within the system. As a result, this weapon can be readily re-equipped at any time for use with optical

Above: The AUG LSW Light Machine Gun.

sights. The special receiver, which permits all optronic or sighting devices to be mounted, can be fitted quickly, and without tools.

The AUG A1 is clearly a preview of the types of infantry weapons that will be used during the twenty-first century, and indeed, the AUG will be among them.

AUG LSW

System type: Light machine gun based on the Steyr AUG A1
Country of origin: Austria
Manufacturer: Steyr-Daimler-Puch AG
Principal distinguishing feature: A light infantry machine gun embodying the versatility of the basic AUG system
Status: Production

In the twenty-first century, small-scale conflicts and anti-terrorist actions will necessitate the acquisition of lighter and lighter infantry weapons which are capable of the high rate of fire usually associated with larger (including fixed) machine guns.

The AUGS HBAR (Heavy Barrel Automatic Rifle) and LSW (LMG Light Machine Gun) reflect the further development of the AUG weapons system. In carrying out this development work, Steyr-Daimler-Puch AG succeeded in producing even this somewhat heavier weapon on the basis of the

already available and well-tried assemblies and components of the AUG system. Moreover, the AUG LSW also meets demands made on small arms by NATO.

The LSW features a slightly heavier barrel with a length of 24 inches, in order to cope with the high thermal stresses of a light machine gun; a special muzzle device, which reduces recoil almost to zero and prevents the weapon from climbing while firing sustained bursts; an adjustable, fold-up bipod fixture; and a magazine, which contains 42 rounds but is also suitable for all other AUG versions. It uses the well-tried Schmidt & Bender four power scope and, of course, any other type of scope, and provides the possibility of using night vision scopes on the same housing. The four power scope has been optimally adapted by the manufacturer to conditions encountered with 5.56mm cartridges. Every other type of optical device can, of course, also be fitted. As a result, the range of the AUG LSW has been extended to more than 2600 feet against individual targets and to approximately 3900 feet against groups of targets.

The LSW features an open bolt to avoid cook off, and carries the AUG standard optical sight. The LSW T uses the open bolt to avoid cook off, and features a rubber-covered, four power scope, which complies with NATO standards. What has been retained in all versions is the economical bullpup design, the use of high-quality synthetic materials, the interchangeability of individual parts within the AUG weapons system and an overall simple design. This results in low weight, a small storage and transport volume, simplification of maintenance work and modest time and expenditure requirements for training purposes in connection with the by the highest operational reliability under weather and use of this weapon. Finally, all LSWs are also characterized environmental conditions of all kinds. To change over from single shots to sustained fire, the shooter must only modify the pressure exerted on the trigger.

As with all other AUG models, the LSW versions can also be rapidly converted into an assault rifle with a 20-inch barrel, a carbine with a 16-inch barrel or a paratroop weapon with a 14-inch barrel. This can be done without impairing their operation simply by changing the barrel.

When the barrel has been sighted, the special receiver can be equipped and stored with any desired optical device such as with a night vision sight. There is no need for renewed sighting-in when the weapon is used later. In addition, the receiver has been equipped with the standardized NATO mounts. However, it can also be fitted without difficulty with all other seats for any available mount. Also, in place of the standard receiver, a specially sealed receiver for water depths of nearly 230 feet is available.

All AUG weapons can be converted, without the use of tools, into a 9mm Parabellum Carbine. This conversion kit consists of barrel group, bolt group, magazine adapter and magazine. The carbine handles like the AUG, but uses the 9mm Parabellum ammunition, but still can take advantage of the built-in optical sight, as well as all other features of the AUG family.

Aurora

System type: Hypersonic transatmospheric aircraft
Country of origin: USA
Manufacturer: Lockheed
Principal distinguishing feature: A secret, extremely fast aircraft with the possible capability of flying into outer space
Status: Unknown, rumored to have been canceled

In the fiscal year 1986, the Department of Defense spent $80 million on project Aurora, and a year later the budget was up to $2.2 billion. Aurora is the project name for a possible replacement for the SR-71 aircraft which may have flown during the late 1980s before being canceled or submerged in another top secret program. Aurora reportedly can be flown at speeds up to Mach 7, and has been observed as a fast, bright light in the sky at 50,000 feet. Aurora is certainly the type of aircraft that represents the leading edge of aviation technology in the early twenty-first century.

B-2

System type: Strategic bomber
Country of origin: USA
Manufacturer: Northrop
Principal distinguishing feature: The largest, longest ranging, stealth aircraft in service
Status: Limited production following initial flight in 1989.

From the time she was first mentioned in public during the 1980 presidential campaign, she had a mystique that went far beyond any facts that we knew about her. If it hadn't

Right: The Northrop B-2 on its sixth test flight in 1989.

been for the fact that President Jimmy Carter desperately needed a weapons system to hang his hat on, she might have remained secret for another decade.

The Reagan Administration brought down the veil of secrecy upon the 'stealth bomber' project, and little more was known for years. By 1985 it was learned that the prime contractor for the mystery ship was Northrop, and this in turn led to speculation that the new airplane would have a 'flying wing' configuration because Northrop's only other heavy bombers had been the YB-35 and YB-49 Flying Wings of the early 1950s.

The B-2 rollout, on 22 November 1988, was the most heavily restricted *public* rollout in history. Indeed, there was a public rollout only because the Air Force decided that it would be impossible to flight test so large an aircraft in total secrecy. Only 500 guests were on hand, and armed guards with German shepherds outnumbered reporters by a ratio of four to one.

The first flight of the strange new airplane began at 6:37 am on 17 July 1989 with Northrop B-2 chief test pilot Bruce Hinds and Air Force Colonel Richard Couch in the cockpit. Much to the chagrin of critics, the flight went smoothly and the big bat touched down lightly at Edwards AFB at 8:29 am. The B-2 differs from the earlier YB-35 and YB-49 in that it has no vertical tail surfaces. Extremely sophisticated, quadruple-redundant, fly-by-wire digital electronic controls had eliminated the need for conventional rudders, as well as resolving the stability problem that was the Achilles heel of the YB-35 and YB-49. Primary flight control consisted of three elevon surfaces on each wing and a rudder/spoiler at each wingtip. The outboard trailing edge had the drag rudder and the next inboard trailing edge surface had two more elevons. This system ingeniously eliminated the need for vertical tail surfaces and made it possible for the B-2 to make turns without a thrust-vectoring system, which some analysts had predicted that the long secret ship would use.

The most unique and important feature of the B-2—indeed its entire purpose for being—is its stealth technology. Stealth is, in fact, a whole basket of technologies designed to make the airplane virtually invisible to radar. These include contours and surfaces that absorb, rather than reflect, radar waves, thus giving the B-2 the radar signature more characteristic of a bird than a B-52.

In terms of actual components, Northrop would build the forward center section (including the cockpit); Boeing (the primary subcontractor) would build the outboard wing section, the landing gear, the aft center section and the bomb bay doors; and LTV (the secondary subcontractor) would build the inboard wing sections, including engine and landing gear housings. The sections built by Boeing included the largest carbon composite aircraft structures ever made. The B-2's radar system is the Hughes ALQ-118, a

Right: The Northrop B-2 stealth bomber prototype touches down at Edwards AFB, California after its initial test flight from nearby Palmdale, California on 17 July 1989.

Rockwell B-1B/Northrop B-2 Range Comparison

For weapon load of eight Short Range Attack Missiles (SRAM) and eight B83 gravity bombs, totaling 37,300 lb.

Aircraft	Fuel Load (lb.)	Takeoff Weight (lb.)	Range (Miles)		
			All High	High-Low-High (1000 Low)	High-Low-High (Optimized)
B-1B with Bay Tank	214,600	444,900	6330	4600	5400
B-1B	196,600	424,900	5800	4100	5170
B-2	160,000	371,330	7250	5060	6100

For weapon load of eight Short Range Attack Missiles (SRAM) and eight B61 gravity bombs, totaling 24,000 lb.

Aircraft	Fuel Load (lb.)	Takeoff Weight (lb.)	Range (Miles)		
			All High	High-Low-High (1000 Low)	High-Low-High (Optimized)
B-1B with Bay Tank	214,600	431,600	6440	4830	5450
B-1B	196,600	411,600	5960	4300	5200
B-2	160,000	358,330	7500	5170	6200

Note: Range is *without* aerial refueling.

penetration and navigation system that also provides target search, detection and track modes.

The first phase of testing was completed in September 1989, and in october the B-2 was flown against a 'Red Team' attempting to detect it using radar which mimicked the state-of-the-art Soviet systems. The second prototype made its initial flight on 19 October and joined the test program.

The only attacks to which the B-2 seemed vulnerable were coming from Washington, DC. In June 1990, the mood in the capital was tempered by the easing of world tensions, and talk had turned to the 'peace dividend.' Budget cutting was the order of the day. Air Force Secretary Donald Rice stated that the service needed a minimum of 75 B-2s, and his boss, Defense Secretary Richard Cheney, cut the order from 132 to 75. In Congress, Les Aspin went one step further and called for killing the program after the 15 aircraft then in existence or in production were complete. This was despite the fact that 40 percent of the budget had already been spent. The 1990-1991 Gulf War and the surprise of the August 1991 Soviet coup did a lot to change America's perception of the need for strategic weapons, but the B-2's most serious challenge is not in the darkened skies over an enemy heartland but in the smoke-filled committee rooms of the nation's capital.

After the collapse of the Soviet Union in December 1991, Congressional pressure increased to force the Air Force to cut the B-2 order from 75 to the 15 which had, at that time, already been authorized. In his 28 January 1992 State of the Union Address, President George Bush stated that '… After completing 20 planes for which we have begun procurement, we will shut down further production of the B-2 bomber.'

Regardless of its political problems, the B-2 remains a technological milestone and a true indication of the shape of the US Air Force—and indeed world air forces—in the twenty-first century.

BILL

System type: Man-portable antitank weapon
Country of origin: Sweden
Manufacturer: Bofors (Bofors Group of Swedish Ordnance after 1991)
Principal distinguishing feature: BILL is the first ground-based antitank rocket to attack tanks from the top
Status: Production

Since the nineteenth century, Bofors has developed and produced defense systems that have consistently amazed military circles throughout the world. From the invention of the ogival screw, that in only two movements achieved a gas-tight sealing of the breech ring, up to the present time of high-tech guns and missile systems, the way has been paved with systems that were first in their field. BILL is no exception.

With a range of 7200 feet, BILL is the first missile system to ever employ the top-attack principle. What happens is that the BILL missile flight path is automatically elevated from the line of sight, enabling the missile to fly clear of all obstacles. The roll-stabilized missile and the downward canted warhead, using a sophisticated combined proximity and impact fuse system, is capable of defeating traditional methods of tank protection.

Above: According to its manufacturer, Sweden's Bofors, 'BILL is easy to use. It's light and easy to carry, can be deployed in 10 seconds in any kind of terrain and has an extremely short reaction time—requiring only five seconds to reload... It is not only its tank and helicopter-defeating capabilities which make BILL the best man-portable, antitank system in the world today, but all those other small, important details that make for effectiveness and increase the fighting man's chances of survival.'

Right: BILL's raisable launcher is completely adaptable to the unevenness of the ground, making it the ultimate attack and ambush system. This also increases BILL's flexibility when combating helicopters or firing uphill or downhill. Whatever firing position is chosen, the system maintains level azimuth. The BILL system presents an extremely small target area with low launch signature, and in night combat situations no visible light emits from the missile. If greater mobility is needed, just integrate it with a vehicle.

BILL was designed to give the soldier in the field a man-portable means of destroying the most advanced types of armor that progressive technology can produce, and do it from almost any position. To fulfill this purpose, BILL has been made light and comfortable to carry, easy to handle, easy to deploy, difficult to detect and given a tank-killing capacity that is out of all proportion to its size. BILL was specifically designed to be easy to operate, and can be deployed, as Bofors explains, 'anywhere there is room for the gunner's knees.'

When firing over water, the guidance system remains unaffected, even if the trailing wire is submerged. The profile, which can be quickly raised or lowered to match the

tactical situation, makes it a formidable standby and ambush weapon. BILL can be made ready, then loaded and reloaded under cover in the fighting position, so that the missile team does not have to expose itself.

While the system is designed for the missile to pass just over the turret roof, the optimized range of the sensor system makes it possible to hit special sections of the target by raising or lowering the aiming point. Low parts of a tank can also be attacked by aiming low and utilizing the impact fuse. In special situations where it would be advantageous to operate without the sensor system—such as where infrared detectors are employed—the gunner can simply switch it off.

Above: BILL is a man-portable antitank system that defeats the most modern main battle tanks by attacking where they are most vulnerable. Traveling at two feet above the gunner's line of sight, BILL overflies the target, and when just in the right position, it strikes down through the roof and devastates the interior!

The BILL missile, which is kept in its sealed launch tube until the moment of firing, is three feet long, 150mm in body diameter and its warhead is canted at 30 degrees to the horizontal. It incorporates a sophisticated proximity sensor system for detecting the target and initiating the shaped charge jet at just the right moment to give maximum effect. There is also an impact fuse for igniting the warhead on a direct hit. Located at the rear of the launch tube is a gas generator, which ejects the missile at a velocity of 236 feet per second. Then the sustainer motor accelerates the missile to 600 feet per second. The sustainer motor burns for approximately two seconds, or 300 yards down range. The missile then continues in free flight, but throughout the time it is gyro-stabilized in roll, keeping the warhead pointing downward.

Brilliant Pebbles

System type: Space-based ICBM interceptor
Country of origin: USA
Manufacturer: TRW/Martin Marietta
Principal distinguishing feature: Probably the most fully developed SDI system
Status: Pre-full-scale development with deployment between 1994 and 2000

In March 1983, President Ronald Reagan outlined a proposal to build a space-based system to defend the United States from an ICBM attack. This program, known as the Strategic Defense Initiative (SDI) is managed by the Strategic Defense Initiative Office (SDIO). Among the technologies investigated by SDIO in its early years were chemical lasers, nuclear-pumped X-ray lasers, neutral particle beams and kinetic energy systems and other weapons using ultra high velocity projectiles. In the late 1980s, several specific kinetic energy projects emerged slightly from behind the veil of secrecy. The leading program seemed to be Brilliant Pebbles, a system utilizing swarms of small, lightweight interceptor projectiles to destroy an ICBM in space. Experiments were conducted, and in June 1991, TRW and Martin-Marietta were given pre-full-scale development contracts. Brilliant Pebbles would be supported by a system of 50 sensor satellites known as Brilliant Eyes.

Above: A nighttime view of the Black Brant X Sounding Rocket used as the launch vehicle for the first two Brilliant Pebbles flight experiments. The rocket has four stages: the terrier (Morton-Thiokol), Black Brant V (Bristol), Nihka (Bristol) and STAR 6B motor (Thiokol). The Terrier (first stage) and Black Brant V (second stage) boost both the target and probe. The STAR 6B motor (fourth stage) propels the probe away from the target for observation. The probe is contained in the silver box just under the nose cone in this photo. The sounding rocket is mounted on the launch rail.

Below: An artist's conception of what a Brilliant Pebbles interceptor might look like. The components include sensors, an inertial measurement unit, propellant tanks, divert thrusters, a computer, batteries and power conditioning. As technologies are explored and developed, the configuration of the actual Brilliant Pebbles interceptor may change.

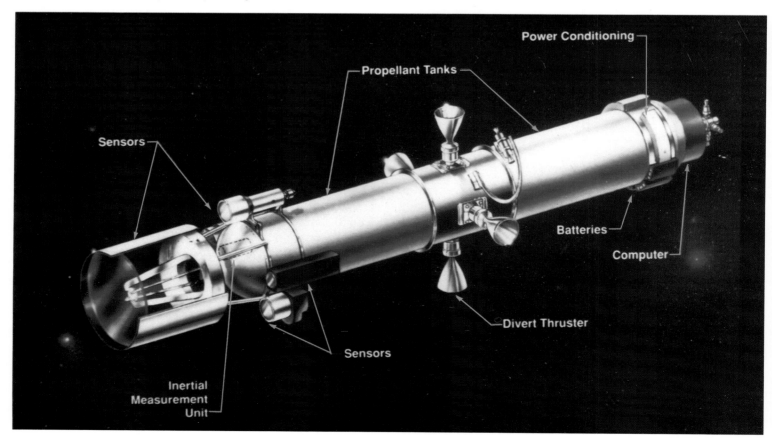

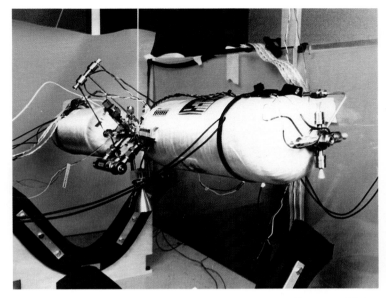

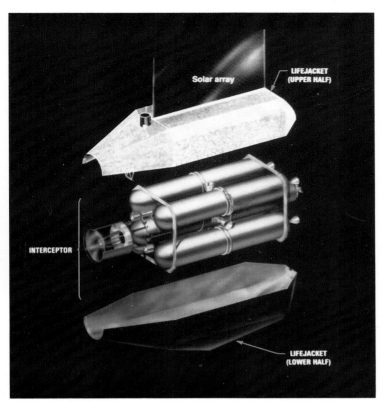

Above: The 'backbone' of this prototype Brilliant Pebbles propulsion system, the twin high-pressure tanks, is lifted from its cushioned supports by action of a computer controlled valve feeding high-pressure gas into the rocket nozzle. It then hovers on this jet and is oriented by intermittent action of its six small computer-controlled thrusters.

Below: Brilliant Pebbles interceptors attack enemy ballistic missiles in the boost phase—when they are still thrusting toward their targets. In this artist's conception, conical-shaped re-entry vehicles are depicted in cutaway. The ballistic missile's first stage booster has just detached and is falling behind the second stage booster. In the distance, both Pebbles have shed their Life Jackets and head toward another target.

Above: An artist's conception of how a Brilliant Pebbles interceptor and Life Jacket might appear. The interceptor, shown in the middle of the illustration, is surrounded by propellant tanks, and fits into the Life Jacket, shown above and below the interceptor. The Life Jacket protects the interceptor while in orbit. In order to accomplish an intercept, the interceptor would leave the Life Jacket and propel to the intended target.

C-17

System type: Tactical airlifter
Country of origin: USA
Manufacturer: McDonnell Douglas (Douglas component)
Principal distinguishing feature: A wide-body, tactical air-lifter that combines large load capacity with the capability of landing on a wide variety of landing fields
Status: Limited production following first flight in 1991 is expected to lead to its being the USAF's workhorse airlifter in the twenty-first century

As became extremely clear in the 1991 Gulf War, combat airlifters in service throughout the world's air forces in the twenty-first century must be capable not only of carrying the largest equipment, but of being able to operate from the roughest of landing fields. The first aircraft to set the standard for these characteristics is the McDonnell Douglas C-17, which McDonnell Douglas began developing for the US Air Force in 1981. Using technology proven on the earlier YC-15 transport, the C-17 will use an externally blown flap system to greatly reduce final approach and landing speeds

for routine, short-field landings. With this powered lift system, the engine thrust is directed to double-slotted flaps to produce additional lifting force. The flaps will be made of titanium, using new technology superplastic forming/diffusion-bonding techniques. The C-17 is designed to be operated by a cockpit crew of two and a single loadmaster. The reduced flight crew complement is made possible through the use of an advanced digital avionics system.

The C-17 combines airlift capability for outsized combat equipment that can now be carried only by the larger Lockheed C-5, and short-field performance now provided only by the Lockheed C-130. This means added airlift not only for direct delivery to austere forward bases, but also for high priority combat mobility within a theater of operations. Only 850 runways in the world can accommodate C-5s and C-141s, while the C-17 can utilize 19,000. In the cargo compartment, the C-17 can carry Army wheeled vehicles in two side-by-side rows, and jeeps can be carried in triple rows. The C-17 is the only aircraft that can airdrop outsized firepower such as the Army's new infantry fighting vehicle. Three of these armored vehicles comprise one deployment load for the C-17. Similarly, the US Army's M1 main battle tank can be carried in conjunction with other vehicles.

The Air Force gave McDonnell Douglas the go-ahead for full-scale development work in February 1985, and the first of an intended total of 120 was rolled out in full camouflage paint scheme in December 1990, with its first flight following on 15 September 1991.

Above: Avionics integration manager Ed Bailey is shown at the controls of the C-17 flight hardware simulator. The C-17 cockpit features stick instead of yoke controls and a head-up-display (HUD) similar to those in fighter aircraft.

Left: The first USAF C-17 airlifter with Pratt & Whitney F117-PW-100 engines running for on-aircraft test procedures at McDonnell Douglas' Long Beach, California, facilities prior to first flight. LTV aircraft division builds the engine nacelles and thrust reversers.

CSH-2 Rooivalk

System type: Combat support helicopter
Country of origin: South Africa
Manufacturer: Armscor
Principal distinguishing feature: A modern attack helicopter designed specifically for low-intensity warfare in the Third World
Status: Full-scale development

A major part of the idea behind the CSH-2 was the South African desire to develop a strong, indigenous capability to design and produce advanced weapons systems. As such, South Africa's case is prototypical of the kind of industries that will emerge in the twenty-first century around the world in countries which have in the past depended on North America and Europe for high-technology weaponry.

The principle factor in the development of this system is simply that the demands of modern, high mobility warfare have dictated the need for a new generation of dedicated combat support systems. In the air support category, this includes combat helicopters, which are designed for full integration with high mobility ground forces. These requirements have been met by the American AH-64 Apache and the Russian Havoc and Hokum types. The next generation will include the RAH-66 Comanche and the new Eurocopter system.

The Rooivalk is the first to appear from this part of the world. Its payload is both formidable and flexible, allowing a combination of air-to-air missiles, laser-guided antitank missiles, 68mm rockets, hydraulically actuated 20 or 30mm cannon, and long-range fuel tanks. Furthermore, due to the MIL-STD-1553B data bus, the Rooivalk weapons platform is generic and can be used for a variety of weapons.

The management of navigational data includes five flight plans containing a total of 100 way points. These flight plans and way points are electronically downloaded at the start of a mission, and may be edited by either crew member during flight. Flight plans are displayed using moving maps.

The detection, identification and tracking of a target is carried out by means of the Target Detection Acquisition and Tracking System (TDATS), comprising a gyro-stabilized turret on which is mounted a FLIR, TV camera, Laser Range-Finder (LRF), Missile Goniometer and a Missile Laser Command Transmitter. A video image 'snapshot' facility is also provided for use during 'pop-up' maneuvers.

Survivability is another key ingredient, as protection of the aircraft against suspended power lines is provided by means of a system of cutters, guides and deflectors. The

CV 90

System type: Armored personnel carrier
Country of origin: Sweden
Manufacturer: Bofors (Bofors Group of Swedish Ordnance after 1991)
Principal distinguishing feature: Vehicle is optimized for rough terrain
Status: Production

Sweden's CV 90 Combat Vehicle is a joint project of Bofors (now part of Swedish Ordnance) and Hagglunds that comprises seven variants. The CV 90 is built around the Bofors 40mm L70 multirole cannon, which carries a 24-round magazine.

The key features of the CV 90 is that it is extremely agile, has a low, very compact structure, minimized radar and infrared signatures, reduced noise levels, and it has a reduced vulnerability to electromagnetic pulses. In addition to the L70, the CV 90 turret mounts a coaxial 7.62mm machine gun and two Bofors LYRAN dischargers for flares and 12 close-range smoke grenade launchers.

The CV 90 is typical of that new generation of tracked—and wheeled—armored vehicles that are designed to be capable of operating in terrain that is potentially impassable for traditional main battle tanks.

CSH-2 is capable of safe, continuous operation for at least 40 minutes following an impact from a B27 12.7mm API projectile. The transmission system is capable of operating for up to 40 minutes following complete loss of oil, with independent engines and fuel and oil tanks, pumping systems and controls. The ammunition bay is able to withstand an impact from a 12.8mm API projectile without detonation. The CSH-2 also employs ballistically tolerant, fire resistant flight controls with redundant load paths. Following the loss of tail rotor control, the tail rotor assumes a position allowing controlled flight, and crashworthy armored seats are provided for both crew members.

The Rooivalk's development has been based on the philosophy of 'if detected—avoid being hit; if hit—avoid crashing; if a crash is unavoidable—ensure crew survival.'

Facing page: The CSH-2 Rooivalk Combat Support Helicopter is capable of assuming a defensive or offensive role. *Center:* The swept-back stub-wings, surface coatings, flat or single curvature surfaces and low main rotor tip speed make the CSH-2 Rooivalk hard to detect by radar, infrared, visual or acoustic signature. *Below:* A new generation tank, the Bofors CV 90.

CARGUS see *Sänger/CARGUS*

Checmate see *Rail Gun Systems*

EAP

System type: Fighter aircraft demonstrator
Country of origin: United Kingdom
Manufacturer: British Aerospace
Principal distinguishing feature: A highly maneuverable aircraft incorporating canard technology
Status: Project terminated, but test results are being used to plan next-generation aircraft

Though the project has since been shelved, the Experimental Aircraft Program (EAP) that originated at British Aerospace (BAe) in 1981 will serve as a foundation for the technology for Britain's twenty-first century fighter aircraft. EAP was originally seen as a successor to the highly successful Panavia Tornado, an aircraft in which British Aerospace had played an important role. As planned, the EAP would not only provide the basis for a future British warplane but the basis for international cooperative projects as well. In fact, both Aeritalia (Alenia after 1990) in Italy and Messerschmitt-Bolköw-Blohm (MBB) in Germany, who were BAe's partners in the Panavia Tornado, were slated to contribute major wing and control surface components to the EAP demonstrator. The EAP aircraft was designed to be powered by a pair of Turbo-Union RB.199 engines, similar to those used on the Tornado, which are also a product of Anglo-Italian-German cooperation.

It was suggested that the production versions of the EAP, if such were to be built, would have been powered by the new Eurojet EJ-200 engines, which were being developed by an international group for use in the European Fighter Aircraft (EFA). As was the case with Turbo-Union, Britain's Rolls Royce is part of the Eurojet consortium. The idea behind the Tornado, and originally behind the EAP, was that tri-national industry would develop and build the aircraft and the air forces of the three nations would buy them. In 1982, however, Germany and Italy withdrew governmental support for the EAP.

Aeritalia and MBB remained involved in the project and both contributed substantially to the EFA. As a result, the EAP demonstrator, which rolled out at Warton, England on 16 April 1986, was not seen so much as a prototype of a specific aircraft, but rather as an amalgam of the technology that would be present in the RAF's fighter fleet—and possibly that of other air arms as well—at the turn of the century, and beyond.

The EAP demonstrator is designed to be capable of a high degree of maneuverability out of a high angle of attack at moderate speed. It is equipped with triple redundant fly-by-wire controls and a state-of-the-art cockpit, which truly displayed the environment in which a twenty-first century pilot would expect to find himself. The EAP made its first flight on 8 August 1986, only one month before it was to become the center of attention at the Farnborough Air Show. Dave Eagles, executive director of flight operations at BAe's Warton facility, piloted the EAP on its debut flight, attaining a speed of Mach 1.1.

The EAP aircraft went on to fulfill an extensive test pro-

Above: This EAP demonstrator made its first flight 8 August 1986. *Facing page:* Considered 'the fighter aircraft of the future,' the EFA is a highly agile, versatile fighter and ground attack aircraft.

gram, the results of which will provide the basic building blocks for the warplanes that will evolve from the joint efforts of British Aerospace and its future twenty-first century partners. Indeed, in 1991 the Advance Studies Department at British Aerospace in Warton began looking at a follow-on to EAP, designated P112, with a Remote Augmented Life System to give it a Short Takeoff, Vertical Landing Capability (STOVL) like the Harrier.

EFA

System type: Lightweight fighter aircraft
Country of origin: Germany/United Kingdom/Italy/Spain
Manufacturer: Eurofighter Jagdflugzeug GmbH
Principal distinguishing feature: A true fifth-generation jet fighter typical of the second generation of multinational cooperative efforts
Status: Full-scale production will follow flight testing if respective national budgets permit

With the European Fighter Aircraft (EFA) as with the British Aerospace EAP, the concept was to build on the experience of the multinational Panavia Tornado project to construct what would amount to a new generation of aircraft designed for the same roles for which the Tornado had been designed more than a decade earlier. After 1982, when Germany and Italy ended their involvement in the cooperative venture which British Aerospace would go on to unilaterally develop into the EAP, there was still a great deal of interest in Europe for a multinational fighter. This interest was not just in the original Panavia countries, but in the Netherlands, Spain and even France, where combat aircraft procurement tended to favor domestic builders to a more substantial degree than anywhere else on the continent.

It was this kind of a potential consortium which United Kingdom Defense Minister Michael Heseltine described at the time as 'impossibly ambitious.' When an agreement was finally reached in August 1985, it was again the Panavia

partners alone who signed. Germany and the United Kingdom each agreed to a 38 percent participation, with Italy underwriting the remaining 26 percent. When the production consortium was formed in June 1986, however, it included not only British Aerospace, Aeritalia (Alenia after 1990) and MBB, but Spain's CASA as well.

In the meantime, United States Defense Secretary Caspar Weinberger had announced in December 1985 that his department would work with the consortium to develop a 'balanced mix of common subsystems' that would also be produced for use on the new American Advanced Tactical Fighter (ATF). The United States would not, however, buy EFA as its ATF because the Americans needed something heavier and longer ranging than that which the Europeans had in mind.

The multinational Eurofighter Jagdflugzeug GmbH consortium was formed in June 1986, and the participants began to define what the EFA would be like and what types of missions it would have to fulfill. They rejected the suggestion made by France that they adapt France's Dassault-Breguet Rafale to meet the EFA requirement. Nevertheless, the full-scale mockup that was shown at the 1986 Farnborough Air Show in September looked a great deal like the Rafale and the British Aerospace EAP demonstrator, both of which were flown publicly for the first time at the show. Ultimately, a great deal of what has been learned from the EAP program will be integrated into the British Aerospace contribution to the Eurofighter. Indeed, the EFA has the same delta airframe and canard control system as the EAP, and it has roughly the same dimensions and gross weight.

The requirements of the participating EFA nations call for a total of about 800 production aircraft, with the production being equitably shared in relation to the number of units ordered by each country. The production of each major subassembly will be allocated as far as possible to a single nation. However, final assembly will take place in all four nations, and all of them will participate in the flight test program. After two years of detailed project definition, full-scale development of the EFA commenced in the beginning of 1988 and will continue until 1999.

Production began with eight prototypes (including two trainer versions), with the first flight scheduled in 1991 at MBB's facility in Manching. MBB would build the first and sixth, British Aerospace the second, third and fifth, and the rest would be divided two and one between Alenia and CASA. To speed the program and reduce risks, initial flight plans involved limited interim use of Turbo-Union RB.199 engines (as used in the Panavia Tornado) until the Eurojet EJ-200 engines become available. A total of more than 2000 hours will be flown by these prototypes before the delivery of the first production aircraft to the nations.

Special attention has been directed towards achieving significant improvements in reliability, availability and operating costs. These aspects have been given the same priority as the achievement of performance parameters. To meet European Staff Requirement the aircraft must be extremely agile and capable of air combat maneuvers not possible in the previous generation of fighters. Special emphasis has therefore been placed on low wing loading, high thrust-to-weight ratio, excellent all around pilot vision and 'carefree handling.' A canard delta layout—similar to that which British Aerospace adopted for the EAP—together with the adaptive control system ensures high levels of both subsonic and supersonic performance. The aircraft's high performance is matched by the attack, identification and defense systems which feature long-range radar and air-to-air missiles. This performance is provided against an expected in-service airframe life of 25 years. The latest computer aided design and manufacturing methods were employed in order to ensure that the objectives of the program were met.

The aircraft is seen by the Eurofighter consortium as the 'fighter aircraft of the future,' one designed to meet the requirements of four major North Atlantic Treaty Organization (NATO) air forces. It has been conceived as a versatile fighter and ground attack aircraft, with a very high performance, coupled with low costs of acquisition and ownership. Its reliability and ease of maintenance provide the high availability required in peace and war, filling not only the needs of the 1990s but those which will exist well into the twenty-first century.

Ekranoplan

System type: Wing-in-Ground Effect (WIG) aerophibious vehicle
Country of origin: USSR (Russia)
Manufacturer: Sukhoi OKB/Beriev OKB
Principal distinguishing feature A revolutionary vehicle that is effectively 'half hovercraft and half airplane'
Status: Initial stages of production

Rumors of the so-called 'Caspian Monster' date back to the 1960s, when a 350-ton WIG was first tested on the Caspian Sea, but it was not until September 1991 that the existence of the Ekranoplan was first confirmed by Soviet authorities. The Soviet (now Russian) Ekranoplan is represented by the

Orlan class vehicles that have been observed in the overall gray livery of the Soviet Navy and the blue and white colors of Aeroflot, the Soviet (now Russian) airline.

Ekranoplans are ships which, like hovercraft, 'fly' on a cushion of air between them and the surface of the water. In the case of the *Orlan* class, two Kuibyshev NK-8 jet engines provide lift by directing their blast downward and aft, under the winglets. Forward motion is delivered by two Kuibyshev NK-12 turboprops mounted in the vertical tail surfaces that drive two huge contra-rotating propellers.

The *Orlan* class vehicles have a cruising speed of 250 mph—much greater than any hovercraft—and a range of 1250 miles. While hovercraft literally *hover* immediately over the surface, Ekranoplans can *fly* up to an altitude of several hundred feet to avoid obstacles.

The *Orlan* class Ekranoplans (designated A.90.150) are 188 feet long, with a payload capacity of over 20 tons and a passenger capacity of up to 150 in a single-deck configuration. A double-decked *Orlan* exists and is capable of carrying 300 passengers. Some of the craft have been configured as offensive warships designed to carry SS-22 anti-ship missiles. The larger *Utka* class Ekranoplans, for example, carry six such weapons. After the collapse of the Soviet Union, Sukhoi was among the most aggressive of design bureaus in looking for civilian markets for its hardware and technology, and talks were initiated with South Korea and Singapore, where 250 mph passenger vessels would have wide potential application. Meanwhile, the military potential of Ekranoplans as patrol and transport craft may well be expanded in the twenty-first century, now that the initial design development and deployment phases have been completed.

Below: An artist's concept of a Russian wing-in-ground effect vehicle powered by eight turbofan engines and firing an anti-ship missile. *Facing page:* A Lockheed YF-22 prototype.

F-22 Lightning/ F-23 Gray Ghost

System type: Fighter aircraft demonstrators leading to deployment as the USAF's fifth generation air superiority jet fighter
Country of origin: USA
Manufacturer: F-22: Lockheed; F-23: Northrop
Principal distinguishing feature: The melding of stealth and supercruise technologies, with a high level of maintainability
Status: Following initial flights by both in 1990, the F-22 was selected by USAF, but F-23 may yet evolve

During the mid-to-late 1980s, the US Air Force was seriously beginning to consider a successor to the McDonnell Douglas F-15, which had been its top air superiority fighter for more than 10 years. Under the program known as Advanced Tactical Fighter (ATF), preliminary proposals were submitted in July 1986 by General Dynamics, Grumman, Lockheed, McDonnell Douglas, Northrop and Rockwell International. The Air Force announced that it would select two contractor proposals and buy two aircraft from each, under the service test designations YF-22A and YF-23A. These aircraft were intended to be flown in competition in 1990-1991, with the winner placed into production, and a total of 750 aircraft to be purchased through 2006. There were five requisites in the design process. The new aircraft would have to incorporate: (1) stealth—low radar-observable—technology; (2) high maneuverability and agility; (3) supersonic cruise without afterburner (*supercruise*); (4) adequate range for all theaters, including the Third World; and finally (5) the capacity to carry at least as much payload as the F-15, but would have to carry it internally, so as not to compromise the clean, clear contours

required of stealth technology. The weapons would include AIM-9 and AIM-120 air-to-air missiles and the M61A1 20mm lightweight, long-barreled Vulcan cannon.

At the same time, the Air Force was evaluating the turbofan engines for use in the winner of the competition. These were the Pratt & Whitney YF119 and the YF120 built by General Electric. One of each of the two competing aircraft would be equipped with one of the two competing engines.

By November 1986, the proposals had been evaluated and Northrop and Lockheed were given parallel $691 million development contracts. The selection seemed to underscore the importance of stealth technology in the ATF program because both of these companies were well into their respective B-2 and F-117 stealth programs at that time. These two contractors in turn teamed up with other 'contestants' to form development teams, with only Grumman and Rockwell not being involved in the ATF work. In the case of the YF-22A, for example, Lockheed would build the forward fuselage and be responsible for the stealth aspects of overall design; Boeing would build the wings, the aft fuselage and offensive avionics; and General Dynamics would complete the mid-fuselage, the control surfaces and the defensive avionics. McDonnell Douglas, which had built the F-15 and had shared the Navy F/A-18 program with Northrop, joined Northrop as the primary subcontractor on the YF-23A.

The centerpiece of the avionics in both ATF contenders' proposals was the Integrated Electronic Warfare System (INEWS). The aircraft themselves will take advantage of the best of the quickly evolving world of fighter aircraft technology to deliver maximum agility, short airfield compatibility and the capability of top speeds above the Mach 1.5 threshold.

Unlike such counterparts in Europe as the Rafale, Gripen or Eurofighter, export marketing was not an important aspect of the ATF's future. However, the US Congress decreed in July 1988 that the US Navy, as well as the US Air Force should participate in the ATF program. Because of the escalating costs of new high technology fighters, Congress intended that whichever aircraft—YF-22A or YF-23A—won the ATF award, it should be able to serve the Navy's needs as well as those of the Air Force. In July 1989, however, it became clear that the naval ATF (NATF) wouldn't be ready for squadron service until the year 2000, so the Navy indicated that it would rather go ahead with the Grumman F-14D, which would be available much sooner. The Navy also recalled the TFX program from the 1960s, which was an earlier, failed attempt to develop an advanced tactical fighter that could serve the needs of both the Air Force and Navy. If the NATF were developed, however, it would add as many as 600 units to the 750 aircraft that the Air Force expects to buy.

The ATF program called for greatly improved reliability and maintainability with high sortie generation rates. The design goal for all areas is twice as good as the F-15 weapon system. The ATF plans also call for an increased survivability rate through a first-look, first-kill opportunity by the use of reduced observables and passive sensors. To decrease the reaction time to enemy threats, increased supersonic cruise and maneuverability goals have been set. To improve operations from battle-damaged runways, the ATF will significantly reduce the take-off and landing distances of that of today's front-line fighters. A greatly increased combat radius, using internal fuel, will allow ATF pilots the upper hand in air superiority.

Extensive use of VHSIC (Very High Speed Integrated Circuits), common modules and high speed databases will be used. The avionics suite will be a highly integrated system which maximizes performance while it minimizes the pilot's workload. Other technologies being evaluated include voice command-control, shared antennas, US military standard ADA software, expert systems, advance data fusion/cockpit display, INEWS, Integrated Communications, Navigation, Identification Avionics (ICNIA) and fiber optics data transmission.

Throughout the process, the configurations remained secret. Artist concepts were not even released until May 1990, shortly before rollouts. The first to be unveiled was the Northrop YF-23A Gray Ghost, which was presented publicly on 22 June 1990. The first YF-23A made its first flight on 27 August, equipped with the YF119 engine. The Ghost subsequently proved to be very smooth and stable in formation flying. The second YF-23A, completed with the

YF120 engine, would make its debut on 26 October. Prior to this, Northrop test pilot Paul Metz had achieved *supercruise* in the YF-23A on 18 September, before the Lockheed YF-22A had made its maiden flight.

The first flight of the YF-22A came on 29 September, with Lockheed test Pilot Dave Ferguson at the controls. The first Lightning II was equipped with the YF120 engine; the second would have the YF119. The YF-22A, unlike its Northrop counterpart, had thrust-vectoring nozzles on its two engines, a factor which would greatly enhance its maneuverability and agility. These were first tested on 15 November. By December it had been shown that the YF-22A consumed one-third less fuel to cruise at supersonic speed than did the F-15.

By the end of December, the two YF-22As had made 74 flights for a total of 92 hours. Both the Lightnings and the Gray Ghosts had live-fired AIM-9 and AIM-120 missiles, and Major Mark Shakelford had flown both airplanes in aerial refueling tests.

The decision on the future of the ATF program was finally reached on 1 May 1991. Air Force Secretary Donald Rice said that the YF-22A and the YF 119 'clearly offered better capability at lower cost, thereby providing the Air Force with a true best value.' Insiders indicated that while the Gray Ghost was faster and perhaps stealthier, the Lightning's thrust-vectoring nozzles had been an important factor, as had been the relative health of the company.

The $98 billion contract would see Lockheed and Pratt & Whitney delivering 648 aircraft (reduced from 750 for budget reasons) between 2001 and roughly 2015. Lockheed would build the Air Force F-22s—and perhaps a US Navy variant—in its Marietta, Georgia facility. By the time the F-22 begins to enter the force, it will have been more than two decades since the introduction of the F-15. The Lightning is the American air superiority fighter of the twenty-first century. It will be designed to be both lethal and survivable while penetrating high-threat airspace. This will be achieved through a proper balance of increased speed and range, enhanced defensive avionics, reduced radar observability and an emphasis on reliability and maintainability.

Below: Northrop's ill-fated YF-23 ATF prototype displayed to news media at Edwards AFB, California in 1990. *Right:* The YF-22 Lightning stealth air superiority jet fighter.

F-117 Nighthawk

System type: Stealth fighter-bomber
Country of origin: USA
Manufacturer: Lockheed
Principal distinguishing feature: The world's first known operational stealth aircraft, the F-117 has an excellent combat record
Status: Operational and likely to remain so while siring follow-on aircraft of the same, or advanced, type

One thing is certain about combat aircraft of the twenty-first century: stealth technology. The star of the 1991 Gulf War was the ugly duckling that happened to be the world's first operational stealth aircraft.

The wars in Vietnam and the Middle East between 1965 and 1975 demonstrated a profound need for fighters and attack aircraft with a low radar cross section that could avoid enemy radar, particularly the radar systems of surface-to-air missiles (SAMs). As early as 1976, this need became a concrete US Air Force development project known as *Have Blue*. By 1977, a prototype aircraft employing 'stealth,' or radar-invisible, technology had been flown. Development of the Lockheed F-117 began in November 1978, and it made its first flight in June 1981. The first group of an eventual 59 F-117s became operational with the 4450th Tactical Group in October 1983 and were assigned to the secret operations center managed by Nellis AFB in the Nevada desert near Tonapah.

It had been widely supposed that this secret aircraft bore the F-19 designation because the Defense Department skipped from F-18 to F-20 in designating nonsecret aircraft. The F-117 designation was used, however, because the aircraft was assigned to the Tonapah site, which operates a number of 'unusual' aircraft designated in pre-1962 'century series' designations (F-112 to F-116, etc).

Built by Lockheed in Burbank, California, the F-117s were

transported to Tonapah at night by C-5 transports for final assembly and training flights. These flights were also conducted at night for the first five years and resulted in two crashes—in July 1986 and October 1987—that were well publicized, although the Air Force refused comment on the aircraft type involved. Indeed, the Air Force didn't even acknowledge the existence of the F-117 until November 1988, when a single photograph was released. This view of the heretofore secret bird was exhibited because the Air Force had decided to fly the F-117 in the daytime, although it would be April 1989 before any of them would be seen and photographed in daylight. The F-117 is powered by a pair of General Electric F404 turbofans and is theoretically capable of supersonic speeds, although it is designed structurally for subsonic missions. It is highly maneuverable and hence is inherently unstable, a fact which led to the adoption of the unofficial, but ubiquitous, nickname 'Wobblin' Goblin.'

In the few years immediately after its unveiling, the F-117 had an amazingly active combat career. In December 1989

during Operation Just Cause, F-117s flew six strikes against Panamanian positions with minimum effectiveness. Six months later, two squadrons of F-117s were deployed to Saudi Arabia as part of Operation Desert Shield.

When Desert Shield became Desert Storm in January 1991, F-117s were the first aircraft to strike Iraq. In fact, it was during Desert Storm that the Nighthawk proved itself to be one of the most extraordinary warplanes ever deployed. Representing only 2.5 percent of the US Air Force assets in the Gulf War, the F-117s nevertheless attacked 31 percent of the targets hit on the first night, assaulting command, control and communications centers in Baghdad, as well as throughout Iraq. During the war, the F-117 hit 40 percent of the strategic targets attacked by Coalition air forces, while having flown only 1.2 percent of the sorties. More amazingly, the F-117 struck its targets with deadly accuracy without being touched by bullets or missiles, or indeed without ever having had any known instance of being tracked by Iraqi radar!

These pages: A 37th Tactical Fighter Wing F-117A photographed by the author at Castle AFB in October 1991.

FS-X

System type: Fighter/fighter-bomber aircraft
Country of origin: Japan
Manufacturer: Mitsubishi/General Dynamics
Principal distinguishing feature: The most advanced combat aircraft to involve design as well as manufacturing contributions by Japanese contractors
Status: Development, with deployment possible by 2000

Japan has relied principally on American-designed aircraft, such as the F-86, F-4 and F-15, since it began to rebuild the air arm of its self defense force in the 1950s, although many of these aircraft have been built in Japan under license from American companies. The only major tactical aircraft designed in Japan since World War II was the Mitsubishi F-1, a ground attack aircraft that had been in service for two decades when the Japanese government started looking for a replacement in 1985. Japan looked at the Panavia Tornado, the General Dynamics F-16 and the McDonnell Douglas F/A-18, but Japanese industry urged the government to consider a domestically produced aircraft instead. In October 1987, Defense Minister Yuko Kurihara and US Secretary of Defense Caspar Weinberger reached an agreement under which Mitsubishi would develop a Fighter Strike, Experimental (FS-X) aircraft for the Japanese Air Self Defense Force (JASDF), which would be based on the General Dynamics F-16, but built in Japan. This agreement was opposed in the United States on the grounds that it would involve the transfer of American technology to Japan. Such opposition failed to take into account that Mitsubishi was *already* building F-15s and that the F-16 technology was more than a decade old. The FS-X will eventually evolve into standard equipment with the JASDF in the early twenty-first century, with nearly 100 in service by that time.

G6

System type: Self-propelled howitzer
Country of origin: South Africa
Manufacturer: Armscor
Principal distinguishing feature: Highly mobile, self-propelled gun
Status: Production

The G6 was developed out of South Africa's years of experience with guerrilla and low-intensity warfare on its northern borders. Intriguingly, this terrain may well duplicate the types of terrain in the Third World upon which the twenty-first century wars may be fought.

A major part of the concept behind the G6 system was the South African desire to develop a strong, indigenous capability to design and produce advanced weapons systems. As such, South Africa's case is prototypical of the kind of industries that will emerge in the twenty-first century around the world in countries which have in the past depended on North America and Europe for high-technology weaponry.

The G6 is a 155mm self-propelled howitzer. It is based on the well-proven ballistic system of the G5 towed gun, and has such indirect fire flexibility that it can be employed in the traditional gun, howitzer and even mortar roles. The gun

Above: The FS-X will become Japan's most advanced combat aircraft by the early twenty-first century. *Below:* The G6 is South Africa's highly-mobile, 155mm self-propelled howitzer.

is mounted on an armored platform driven by six wheels, and is capable of speeds in excess of 50 mph, making it ideally suited to supporting the movement, deployment and action of mechanized infantry and armored divisions. High-strength armor steel protects the six-man crew against small arms fire, and allows the vehicle to pass through densely shrubbed terrain. Its main weapon is a 155mm auto-fret-taged .45 caliber gun. 155mm is a preferred artillery caliber, providing maximum range and striking power within the limits of reasonable handlability. A 12.7mm machine gun is fitted to the cupola as a secondary weapon, and is capable of firing up to 750 rounds per minute. Eight 81mm launchers are mounted on the turret to fire smoke grenades for the generation of smoke screens.

Sophisticated electronic navigation and north-finding equipment is currently under development for integration into the fire control system. This will give the G6 fully autonomous navigation capability, thereby significantly decreasing reaction time.

Galil ARM/AR/SAR

System type: 5.56mm Assault rifle series
Country of origin: Israel
Manufacturer: Israel Military Industries (IMI)
Principal distinguishing feature: Designed to be an all-weather, all-environment infantry assault weapon
Status: Production

Few armsmakers have the same reputation for reliability that IMI has. Its Uzi weapons are well known, and the Galil is a model for the types of infantry weapons that will prevail in the twenty-first century. The Galil is lightweight, air cooled, gas operated and magazine fed. It can be fired from the hip or shoulder in an automatic or semiautomatic mode. All three models of the Galil are available for use with NATO-recommended SS109, 5.56mm cartridges.

The Galil 5.56mm-Model ARM is an assault rifle and light

machine gun with a bipod and carrying handles; the Galil 5.56mm-Model AR is a fully automatic assault rifle, the basic infantry weapon; and the Galil 5.56mm-Model SAR is a fully automatic, short-barreled assault rifle, ideal for tank crews, airborne troops and commandos. The Galil Model ARM is one of very few assault rifles with a built-in bipod. The Galil's bipod is strong, won't break or deform when slammed on the ground and contains a wire cutter. Overall lengths for the ARM, AR and SAR, respectively are 38.6 inches, 38.6 inches and 33.1 inches. The maximum rate of fire for all three is 650 rpm. Rifling for these three Galil models is right handed, one turn in 12 inches.

Galil alone among the major assault rifles in the 1980s had foldable night sights (tritium light). In addition, only the Galil has a built-in base for accommodating almost all types of sight and SLS mounts. A special night safety catch, featured only on the Galil, permits the shooter to retract the cocking knob and open the receiver without putting a round in the chamber from the magazine. The chamber is directly in front of the ejection port, allowing the shooter to finger check (in the dark) for the presence of a round and close the receiver, leaving the chamber empty. The Galil breaks down into a mere five parts with no pins or other small parts that could be easily lost in the dark.

The Galil has a three-position fire selector lever: safe, semiautomatic and fully automatic. When in safe position, the fire selector lever completely blocks the trigger and covers the slot in which the cocking handle travels, thus preventing cocking of the weapon and preventing dirt from entering the mechanism.

Right: The Galil Sniper Rifle offers a high level of accuracy.
Below: The 7.62mm semi-automatic Galil in the field.

Galil Sniper Rifle

System type: Semiautomatic rifle
Country of origin: Israel
Manufacturer: Israel Military Industries (IMI)
Principal distinguishing feature: The weapon delivers a high level of accuracy
Status: Production

A variation on the 7.62mm Galil of the 1970s and a cousin of the Galil AR series, the Galil Sniper Rifle is a semiautomatic, gas operated rifle, with a rotating bolt fed from a 20-round magazine and firing M-118, FN Match or any other standard NATO 7.62 x 51mm ammunition. The shot grouping possible with this very accurate firearm is within a circle of 4.7 to 5.9 inches diameter at 328 yards. This is possible thanks to three important features: a special heavy barrel, location of the bipod on the receiver, and the design of the telescopic sight mount and its attaching slide on the receiver.

H-2

System type: Manned spaceplane
Country of origin: Japan
Manufacturer: NASDA
Principal distinguishing feature: Japan's first manned spacecraft
Status: Development, with deployment after 2000

By the early twenty-first century, Japan intends to have a manned space flight capability equal to any. Like the Hermes spaceplane being developed in France, Japan's H-2 Orbiting Plane (HOPE) is a small, two-person spaceplane based on the Boeing X-20 of the 1960s, although in August 1990, there was some discussion of doubling the size. Engineered and built by Mitsubishi, the HOPE was first seen in preliminary form in March 1987, and a full-scale mockup was displayed at the 1989 Paris Air Show. HOPE will be placed into orbit from the Japanese National Space Development Agency's (NASDA) Space Center at Tanegashima using an H-2 heavy lift booster rocket. Its potential landing sites include Kagoshima, near Tanegashima, and several other places in Japan, as well as Christmas Island and Australia's Cape York.

Right: HOPE is expected to land in Kagoshima, having achieved orbit using a booster rocket (*below*).

Have Slick

System type: Air-launched standoff
Country of origin: USA
Principal distinguishing feature: A composite missile with stealth characteristics
Status: In development

Have Slick was in development as early as 1990, designed to be a future weapon for use in the F-117, F-22 and B-2, as well as F-16 and F-15E. It is described as being like a 'shotgun shell,' capable of carrying a variety of submunitions.

HEDI

System type: Atmospheric ICBM interceptor
Country of origin: USA
Manufacturer: McDonnell Douglas
Principal distinguishing feature: Kinetic energy kill vehicle
Status: Development and testing in the early 1990s

In March 1983, President Ronald Reagan outlined a proposal to build a space-based system to defend the United States from an ICBM attack. This program, known as the Strategic Defense Initiative (SDI) is managed by the Strategic Defense Initiative Office (SDIO). Among the technologies investigated by SDIO in its early years were kinetic energy systems, a genre of weapons that use high speed projectiles to destroy ICBMs. In the late 1980s, several specific projects emerged slightly from behind the veil of secrecy.

The McDonnell Douglas High Endoatmosphere Defense Interceptor (HEDI) missile was developed as part of the Kinetic Kill Vehicle Integrated Technology Experiments (KITE). It was first launched in January 1990 to determine whether an infrared homing seeker could intercept ICBM warheads entering the atmosphere while surviving the heat of high closing velocities. The first HEDI test experienced premature warhead separation, but the test objectives were listed as 95 percent accomplished.

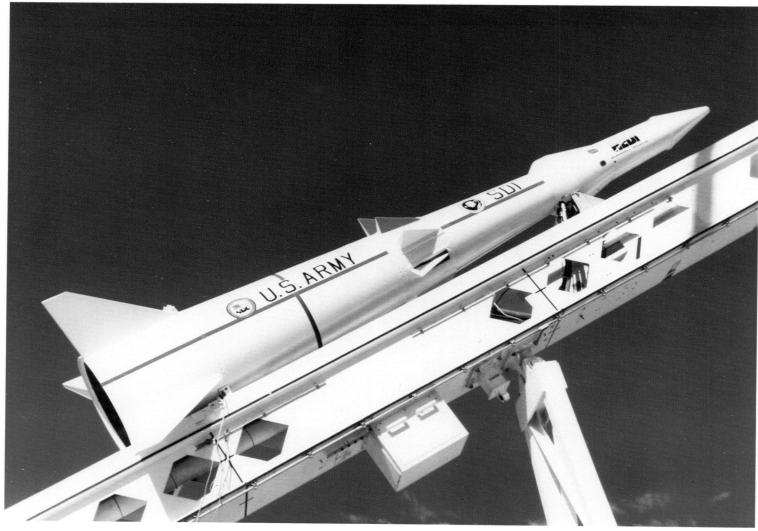

Left, above: The launch of the US Army's HEDI on 26 January 1990. *Facing page:* Two views of the first of the HEDI project's KITE vehicles, KITE-1, at White Sands Missile Range. *Below:* Ariane 5, Hermes and the space station Columbus are designed for commercial missions in the twenty-first century. *Below, right:* Hermes can carry a crew of three.

Hermes

System type: Manned spaceplane
Country of origin: France
Manufacturer: Dassault-Breguet/Aerospatiale
Principal distinguishing feature: The first French manned spacecraft, and probably the first outside the USA or USSR
Status: Development, with deployment by 2000

After several years of preliminary studies, Philippe Couillard of France's National Center for Space Studies (CNES) announced in October 1985 that France's two largest aircraft builders, Dassault-Breguet and Aerospatiale, had been selected to collaborate on the development of the Hermes spaceplane. After 35 years of the Soviet Union and the United States having a monopoly on spacecraft capable of carrying human beings, France will be the first of several nations to develop an independent means of sending humans into space.

Dassault-Breguet would be responsible for the aerodynamics, airframe, flight testing and re-entry trajectory. Aerospatiale would plan the cockpit, avionics, power system and orbital operations. Approximately half of the total subsystems would be drawn from other European countries, such as Austria, Belgium, Denmark, Italy, the Netherlands, Sweden and Switzerland, which were partners with France in the European Space Agency (ESA). Germany did not join the Hermes project initially because of prior commitments to its own Sänger spaceplane project.

With a length of 52 feet and a wingspan of 33 feet, the two-man Hermes spaceplane is less than half the size of the American Space Shuttle or Soviet *Buran* Orbiter, but it is very close in size and configuration to the American Boeing X-20 spaceplane, which was built but never flown in the 1960s. A full-scale mockup of Hermes was unveiled at the Paris Air Show in June 1987, and it is expected to be in full operation by the turn of the century. It will be capable of commuting to both American and Soviet space stations and of flying independent missions to launch satellites from its payload bay. The Hermes vehicle is prototypical of a type of small spaceplane, which was predicted to come into service as early as the 1960s, but which will be part of routine space operations in the twenty-first century.

HL-20 (PLS)

System type: Personnel space launch system
Country of origin: USA
Manufacturer: NASA Langley
Principal distinguishing feature: A lightweight, low-cost system for carrying personnel between the earth and space
Status: In development, mock-up presented in 1990

When the NASA Space Shuttle was being developed in the early 1970s, one of its principle missions was to carry personnel to the large space station that NASA intended to have in place by the early 1980s. The space station project was postponed, and the Shuttle became the only means NASA had for conducting manned missions in space.

By the end of the 1980s, the Space Station *Freedom* was being designed and NASA began to look at concepts for a miniature Space Shuttle, or, as NASA itself called it, 'a small space taxi system.' This system would be capable of carrying material and up to 10 people to and from the Space Station.

Developed by the NASA Langley Research Center, the HL-20 is one of two concepts being considered by NASA as a Personnel Launch System (PLS). The system would assure rapid, manned access to space and minimize maintenance costs. Like the X-20 of the 1960s or the French Hermes spaceplane, the PLS would be launched from an expendable booster and would be capable of conventional runway landings. With its wings folded, the HL-20 PLS could also fit within the Shuttle's payload bay.

If it flies, the HL-20 would be the fifth manned spacecraft operated by the United States and the first to go into service since 1981. As space operations become more routine in the twenty-first century, systems like the HL-20 will be extremely useful, and certainly easier and cheaper to use, than the larger Space Shuttle System.

Above and opposite: Unveiled on 21 September 1990, the HL-20 PLS full-scale engineering model in this photograph is 29.5 feet long and 23.5 feet across the wingspan. It was built by students and faculty members at North Carolina State University at Raleigh, North Carolina, and by North Carolina Agricultural and Technical State University at Greensboro, North Carolina. The HL-20 model will be used at NASA Langley and at the NASA Johnson Space Center at Houston, Texas, to study crew seating arrangements, habitability, equipment layout, crew ingress and egress and maintenance and handling operations.

HOE

System type: Ground-based ICBM interceptor
Country of origin: USA
Manufacturer: Lockheed
Principal distinguishing feature: The system uses the unique 'fan' to increase its kill ratio
Status: Tested development project

The US Army's Homing Overlay Experiment (HOE) is a Strategic Defense Initiative kinetic energy weapon designed to use a unique system of unfurlable fan blades to increase its kill ratio. In 1984, a HOE interceptor was used against an actual incoming ICBM. A target missile was launched from Vandenberg AFB, California, on a flight path which closely resembled the trajectory of an intercontinental ballistic missile. The course of the missile took it west over the Pacific. A nonnuclear interceptor was launched from the Kwajalein missile range in the central Pacific. For reference, Kwajalein is in the Marshall Island chain, approximately 6000 miles away from the launch site in California. While the drone ICBM was on its trajectory, the interceptor was accelerated to a speed of more than 10,000 mph. When the radar at Kwajalein acquired the target, the interceptor was directed toward it and given final automatic control of the intercept.

The HOE's upper stage (the homing and kills stage) included long wavelength, infrared detection and homing techniques for in-flight guidance to the target. Prior to contact with the target, the interceptor unfurled a metal, ribbed array structure with a diameter of about 15 feet. Because of the closure speed of the two objects (nearly 30,000 mph) there was no need for an explosive device on the interceptor. When the two missiles made contact at an altitude of about 90 miles above the Pacific, they had a combined closure speed of about 5.5 miles per second (almost 20,000

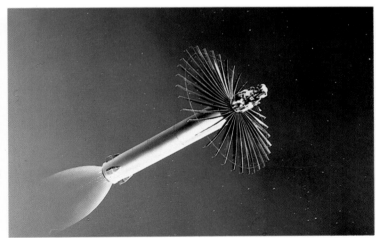

Above: The Army Homing Overlay Experiment (HOE), shown in this illustration, won Lockheed Missiles & Space Company, its designer and builder, the 1986 Strategic Defense Technical Achievement Award after totally destroying an aggressor ICBM more than 100 miles above the earth in a 1984 test mission — a feat akin to, as one authority put it, 'hitting a bullet with a bullet.' Once launched, the Earth-based HOE locked onto its target using its tracking sensor (the interceptor's prominent nose), and unfurled its kill-radius increasing 'fan' en route to closing with the speeding ICBM at over 15,000 feet per second.

mph), and the force of the impact destroyed both missiles.

The intercept of the ICBM was quite significant for defense system planners. It showed that the technology was available to 'kill' offensive threats in the late boost through midcourse phases of a ballistic missile trajectory. The precision of the event was particularly impressive. Knocking out a missile at an altitude of something better than 100 miles is akin to 'shooting a bullet with a bullet.'

HOPE see *H-2*

HORUS see *Sänger/CARGUS*

HOTOL

System type: Single-stage-to-orbit (SSTO) spaceplane
Country of origin: United Kingdom
Manufacturer: British Aerospace
Principal distinguishing feature: Potentially Britain's first manned spacecraft
Status: Serious study, dormant in the late 1980s, but revived in 1990

The British Aerospace Horizontal Takeoff & Landing (HOTOL) spaceplane has been on the drawing board since the early 1980s, and in April 1986, the company sought to have the craft adopted as the European Space Agency's (ESA) official spaceplane. It was to be powered by the Rolls Royce RB5454 engine developed by Alan Bond. An air-breathing rocket, the RB5454 uses liquid hydrogen and liquefied air for speeds up to Mach 5.5, and onboard liquid hydrogen and oxygen for faster speeds and flight above 100,000 feet. Meanwhile, however, the French Hermes, a simpler spacecraft that happened to be more fully developed at the time, received the honor of having the flags of the ESA member nations painted on its fuselage.

The HOTOL project was put on the back burner for several years then revived in 1991 in the 0068 configuration, which had about the same overall dimensions as the United States Space Shuttle Orbiter, but with a much a larger fuselage volume. The deployable vertical, stabilized foreplane, which gave earlier HOTOL configurations a sort of 'catfish-like' appearance, was still present.

Also in 1991, British Aerospace began discussions with the Soviet Union's Central Aero-Hydromanics Institute (TsAGI) and the Antonov Design Bureau on the huge Antonov An-225 (see page 14) to air launch the HOTOL vehicle. This would involve the An-225 carrying the HOTOL to 30,830 feet, going into a power dive to 28,860 feet, pulling up abruptly and releasing the spaceplane at 30,000 feet. The HOTOL would ignite its four engines four seconds later and roar into space. Meanwhile, British Aerospace was working with the Chemical Automatics Design Bureau in Voronezh to develop the HOTOL's RD-120 power plant.

In January 1992, wind tunnel tests began at TsAGI in the T117 hydrosonic tunnel, which involved the HOTOL *with* the An-225 and alone. The latter configuration was studied at speeds of Mach 10.5 to Mach 14, providing the thermodynamic heating data to determine the location of HOTOL's vertical stabilizer.

The initial HOTOL missions would be flown, unmanned, from the ESA launch facility at Kourou, French Guyana, but could theoretically be launched from any long runway in

the world. The HOTOL was designed to carry payloads of up to nine tons, so the An-225 would need an especially long runway and two additional engines (as shown *above*).

HYTEX see *Sänger/CARGUS*

JAS-39 Gripen

System type: Fighter/fighter-bomber aircraft
Country of origin: Sweden
Manufacturer: SAAB-Scania
Principal distinguishing feature: The most advanced aircraft in Europe at the time of its first flight in 1988
Status: Flight testing following resumption of program in 1990, with deployment by 2000

With the awesome firepower of the Warsaw Pact less than 30 minutes flying time from anywhere in Sweden, the Swedish defense establishment had always maintained a vigilant defense posture. Furthermore, in order to safeguard its neutrality, which it maintained even throughout World War II, Sweden has nurtured and developed an independent domestic arms industry. This has included the SAAB family

Above: An artist's concept of the British HOTOL spaceplane being launched from an 8-engine An-225. *Below:* The JAS-39 Gripen is noted for speed and maneuverability.

of first-line combat aircraft, which went into production just after World War II, and has culminated at the end of the century with the SAAB-Scania JAS-39 Gripen (Griffon), conceived as the twenty-first century successor to the SAAB-Scania JA-37 Viggen (Thunderbolt), which entered service with the Swedish air force (Flygvapnet) in 1971. It was developed to perform in the fighter, attack and reconnaissance roles. Potential export customers included Denmark and Finland, who had both bought earlier SAAB fighter aircraft, and who are natural customers because they share the terrain and weather conditions for which SAAB optimized its warplanes. Because of the rugged Scandinavian topography and the possibility that conventional airfields would be destroyed early in a potential conflict, the Gripen is designed for high reliability and simple maintenance. In the field, conscript technicians can quickly prepare the aircraft for the next flight. The Gripen has an Auxiliary Power Unit and a comprehensive, built-in test system. It also offers the possibility of a new basing concept which uses dispersed road bases or small airfields.

The JAS-39 was rolled out at Linkoping, Sweden on 26 April 1987, SAAB's fiftieth birthday. The first flight, however, was delayed by avionics software development until 9 December 1988, when SAAB's chief test pilot, Stig

Holmstrom, took the Gripen up to 21,000 feet at Mach .8 on the maiden flight. The program suffered a serious setback when the first prototype was involved in a crash during its sixth flight on 2 February 1989. As the second prototype had not yet been completed, this left SAAB without a demonstrator, which was essential in lining up the export customers vital to the financial success of the program. Nevertheless, the show continued, with the second prototype flying in May 1990, followed by a third in December 1990 and a fourth (actually the third to be built) in March 1991.

By the time the program was back on track in May 1991, the second prototype had flown 51 times—once a week for a year—and the fourth (third to fly) had made 19 test flights. Delivery of the first production series of 30 Gripens to the Swedish air force will begin in the late 1990s. The total requirement, as estimated by the supreme commander of the Swedish armed forces, will be 21 to 23 squadrons, or 350 to 400 aircraft, although the initial order involved only 110 aircraft.

The combat scenarios of the twenty-first century will be characterized by extensive electronic warfare and concentrated attacks on airfields and communications centers, so the Gripen has been designed to survive with full operational capability under such conditions. As well as being difficult to detect on the ground and in the air due to low signatures, the aircraft also has comprehensive countermeasures equipment and a high ability to operate in a combat environment.

Flight characteristics and performance on the Gripen are designed for fighter missions with high demands on speed, acceleration and maneuverability. The combination of delta wing and all moving canard gives it excellent takeoff, flight performance and landing characteristics. These are achieved through a fly-by-wire control system with built-in redundancy. This gives the aircraft outstanding maneuverability and safety, as well as enabling it to carry a wide variation in payload. The JAS-39 weighs only half as much as its forerunner, the JA-37 Viggen, but can carry the same weapons load. This has been accomplished through developments in materials, avionics and engine technology.

Keyhole

System type: Digital reconnaissance satellite series
Country of origin: USA
Manufacturer: US Air Force
Principal distinguishing feature: Can read license plates from geosynchronous orbit
Status: Operational, with more advanced series spacecraft in development

The US Air Force operates a network of reconnaissance satellites, the best known of which are the Keyhole series, which include the 14-ton KH-9 Big Bird satellites deployed since the early 1970s. With a lifespan of six months, the Big Bird could remain on station six times longer than its Russian equivalents. Big Bird automatically photographed its targets, and returned television pictures or film packs for recovery and processing. More advanced reconnaissance satellites are the KH-11 and KH-12 series. First deployed in 1978, they have a two-year lifespan and far more sensitive equipment than Big Bird. The satellites carry powerful cam-

eras and infrared sensors, and are equipped to return their information in digital form. The infrared system reportedly allows it to 'photograph' events that have taken place in the recent past via extremely sensitive sensors that detect minute amounts of residual heat. During the 1991 Gulf War, data provided by the Keyholes proved invaluable to American and Coalition forces in the Middle East.

Kinetic Energy Interceptor

System type: Space-based ICBM interceptor
Country of origin: USA
Manufacturer: Martin Marietta or Rockwell International
Principal distinguishing feature: Highly accurate kinetic energy system
Status: In development with potential deployment by 2000

In March 1983, President Ronald Reagan outlined a proposal to build a space-based system to defend the United States from an ICBM attack. This program, known as the Strategic Defense Initiative (SDI) is managed by the Strategic Defense Initiative Office (SDIO).

Among the technologies investigated by SDIO in its early years were kinetic energy systems, which are weapons that use high-speed projectiles to destroy ICBMs in space. In the late 1980s, several specific projects emerged slightly from behind the veil of secrecy. The leading program seemed to be Brilliant Pebbles, a kinetic system utilizing swarms of small, lightweight interceptor projectiles. The principal competitor to Brilliant Pebbles was the Kinetic Energy Interceptor project being developed by Rockwell International and Martin Marietta. The first demonstration of this type of system came in August 1989 (*right*) when a Martin Kinetic Kill vehicle, lifted by lateral rocket thrusters, flew for 13.5 seconds in a hanger at Edwards AFB and used an infrared sensor to track its target. Tests conducted by Rockwell a year later suggested that a 200 pound Space-Based Interceptor (SBI) could be scaled down to 20 pounds and could achieve an accuracy that was likened to being able to shoot a basket from a mile away. In 1990, SDIO considered the Kinetic Energy Interceptors, or SBIs, could be parked in orbiting 'garages,' as an alternative to Brilliant Pebbles, which involved independently orbiting interceptors.

LEAP

System type: Space-based ICBM interceptor
Country of origin: USA
Manufacturer: Boeing Space Systesm (primarily), as well as Hughes and Rockwell
Principal distinguishing feature: Simple, lightweight projectile system
Status: Development

Among the Strategic Defense Initiative technologies investigated by the Strategic Defense Initiative Office (SDIO) are such kinetic energy weapons as Brilliant Pebbles, the Kinetic Energy Interceptor project and the High Endoat-

Above: The 1990 miniaturized Martin Space-Based Interceptor (SBI) Kinetic Kill vehicle during a hover test as it tracks its intended target.

Left: A facsimile of the Martin SBI projectile, during a test on 24 April 1989.

Below: A smaller version of the prototypical SBI hover test vehicle at Edwards AFB, California, 31 July 1990.

These pages: The MiG-29 was the first Soviet fighter designed with an aerodynamically blended wing fuselage transition.

mosphere Defense Interceptor (HEDI) missile. While HEDI is designed for use *within* the atmosphere, the Lightweight Exoatmospheric Projectile (LEAP) program was designed to be based in space.

Prior to the existence of LEAP, only liquid fuel systems were believed small enough to fit in a lightweight weapon and at the same time remain accurate during rapid pulsing required to intercept and destroy a target. In January 1992, LEAP program manager Richard Matlock announced that the system 'now enables solid propellants to be used for applications where we are providing precise control for a projectile to maneuver to hit a target.'

On November 1991, a 13-pound LEAP demonstrator vehicle was tested at the Thiokol facility at Elkton, Maryland. At a simulated altitude of 100,000 feet, it fired 4000 degree F gases from 10 thrusters at a rate of fire of 200 times per second for 37 seconds.

After the tests, SDIO and the US Navy began discussions of a LEAP-based theater defense weapon, and the Navy's Lockheed Trident missile was suggested as a launch vehicle. It is interesting to note that the huge Trident has a 13:1 thrust-to-weight ratio, while LEAP has a 120:1 thrust-to-weight ratio.

MiG-29

System type: Fourth generation jet fighter aircraft
Country of origin: USSR
Manufacturer: Mikoyan OKB
Principal distinguishing feature: Versatile and easily maintained fourth generation aircraft
Status: Operational since mid-1980s, and likely to remain so well into the twenty-first century

Artyem Mikoyan and Mikhail Gurevich formed the aircraft design bureau (OKB) that bears their name in 1939. After a series of relatively insignificant aircraft during World War II, the team succeeded in developing the Soviet Union's finest first-generation jet fighter, the MiG-15. This aircraft was followed by the similar, though somewhat larger, MiG-17, the supersonic MiG-19 and the ubiquitous MiG-21.

In the early 1980s, the Mikoyan OKB (the Gurevich name is no longer used, although the abbreviation is still MiG) set about to design a true fourth-generation fighter, an effort which succeeded very well. The MiG-29 (NATO codename Fulcrum) is a twin-engined fighter with a high thrust-to-weight ratio that is significantly improved over earlier MiGs. Similar in size and configuration to the American F/A-18, the MiG-29 is the first Soviet fighter designed with an aerodynamically blended wing fuselage transition.

The MiG-29 was first seen by Western 'observers' at the Ramenskoye test facility in March 1979, and it entered squadron service six years later. It made its first appearance in the West in July 1986 during a visit to Rissala AB in Finland. In September 1988, a MiG-29 and a MiG-29U (*Uti*) trainer made a surprise visit to the Farnborough Air Show in Britain, where they presented an aerobatic display that left the audience very impressed with the aircraft.

A twin-engined fighter with a positive thrust-to-weight ratio, the MiG-29 is powered by two Isotov RD-33 turbofans. It is the first high-performance Soviet aircraft to make extensive use of blended contour carbon fiber composite structural components.

Prior to 1992, the Soviet Union operated more than 500 MiG-29s, with those being assigned chiefly to the western Soviet Union and along the Sino-Soviet border. Also contained in these numbers are perhaps 100 MiG-29U trainers. Export customers include Cuba, India, Iraq, North Korea, Syria and Yugoslavia. Czechoslovakia and East Germany were the only Warsaw Pact users, and in 1990 when Germany was reunified, the former East German MiG-29s—much to our surprise—were transferred to the Luftwaffe rather than being confiscated by Moscow. They will be the only East German aircraft *retained* by the Luftwaffe, the other types being sold or scrapped. There was also some discussion in 1991 about the Luftwaffe selling MiG-29s to the US Navy for aggressor training, but that deal was never pursued because of the high cost of maintaining the MiGs in the United States.

By the time of the collapse of the USSR in December 1991, MiG-29s had generally replaced older types in the Soviet arsenal. Production for service in the post-USSR Russian air force was terminated in 1992 for budgetary reasons, but MiG-29s are likely to remain as the backbone of Russian, Ukrainian and Byelorussian air power well into the twenty-first century. At the same time, the Mikoyan OKB will be looking aggressively at the export market.

Particle Beam Weapons

System type: ICBM interceptors
Country of origin: USA/former USSR
Manufacturer: Various
Principal distinguishing feature: These systems use beams of sub-atomic particles to destroy ICBMs and other targets
Status: Experimental

In early twentieth century pulp science fiction, heroes and villains alike used 'death rays' to destroy their adversaries. In the twenty-first century, 'death rays' will become a reality. In fact, they already exist in the form of the directed energy experiments being undertaken by the Strategic Defense Initiative Office (SDIO) of the US Department of Defense, as well as in the Soviet Union.

By definition, particle beam weapons are systems which rely on the technology of particle accelerators to emit beams of charged or neutral particles which travel at nearly the speed of light. Such a beam could theoretically destroy a target by several means, including electronic disruption, softening of metal and explosive destruction. These weapons differ from Kinetic Kill Vehicles, such as Brilliant Pebbles, in that they use beams of particles rather than tangible projectiles.

The neutral particle beam is a space-based weapons concept utilizing accelerated negative ions as the disruptive energy force. The neutral particle beam weapons envi-

sioned would be configured much like the space-based lasers. A series of these weapons would be placed in an orbital network, where they would be capable of engaging ballistic missile boosters and postboost vehicles as their launch trajectories lifted them out of the atmosphere.

A particle beam weapon can disable a missile without actually destroying it. The beam of charged particles would not burn a hole in the skin of a missile as would a laser beam. Instead, the particle beam would easily pass through the skin of a vehicle and disrupt the electronic devices on board. Neutral particle beams are effective at altitudes of about 90

Above: A technician inspects equipment that is part of Los Alamos National Laboratory's neutral particle beam weapon experiment. *Below:* In this conception, a space-based neutral particle beam 'gun' destroys hostile ICBMs.

miles. More importantly, neutral particle beams offer the promise of efficient boost-phase destructive force. SDI planners are definitely interested in the fact that particle beam weapons have an unlimited stream of energy. Because of this (and the fact the beams penetrate through the target), these weapons do not need to dwell on targets like lasers. Much of our base knowledge regarding neutral particle beams comes from the USSR. Soviet scientists have been studying this area of science for some time. Indeed, their research literature included extensive discussions about their research efforts. Apparently they became aware of the potential sensitivity of the research, and in the early 1970s they suddenly stopped reporting on the subject.

Particle beam weapons would use an accelerator to speed up a stream of negative ions to a velocity near the speed of light. These particles are driven down the length of the accelerator by using electromagnetic fields. The negative ions are drawn even faster by the speed of on-off switching of the electromagnetic fields. Near the end of the accelerator, a final series of magnets 'point' the particle beam at the target. Prior to leaving the weapon, though, one final step is required: the ions are stripped of their negative charges. This is a key step in the process. If the negative charges were not taken away, the negative ions in the beam would repel one another, and the beam would become diffused. Further, negative ions in the beam could be attracted to the earth's magnetic field, and as a result would be deflected from their intended target.

Although designed as a weapons system, the space-based particle beam stations could also provide a sensor function for the defense system during the postboost and midcourse phases of a missile trajectory. It appears that when an object is 'hit' by a particle beam, it emits gamma rays and neutrons. The gamma rays and neutrons released seem to be in proportion to the size and mass of the object. With this in mind, these emissions could be be used to discriminate between lightweight decoys and heavier re-entry vehicles.

Particle beam technology could also provide the same destruction as lasers. Depending upon what sort of particles are used (there are many choices: electrons, protons, hydrogen atoms, etc), the beam can have a physical impact as well as an electrical one. This physical impact would be quite destructive because of the near-light speed velocity of the beam. Particle beams of the future may have the capability of either physically destroying a target or disabling it by way of electronic disruption.

There is no doubt that the particle beam technology weapons concept can be represented in some future version of a defense system. Experimentation in this technology is proceeding quite successfully. Recently, scientists developed and successfully tested the radio-frequency quadruple preaccelerator. This device accelerates a charged ion beam. This development is considered a major improvement in particle beam technology. Experiments have also produced an ion beam with qualities superior to SDI design goals. Also, scientists have demonstrated a method for precision aiming of a neutral beam. Testing will continue. The Neutral Particle Beam (NPB) Technology Integration experiment is designed to investigate the technologies needed to perform midcourse discrimination or to detect nuclear material. This experiment will be conducted in space at low power levels and use nearby co-orbital instrumented targets. In compliance with the 1972 ABM Treaty, the device will not be capable of autonomously acquiring or tracking ballistic missile targets. The NPB Midcourse Discrimination Technology experiment will eventually require the use of the Space Shuttle.

While an actual particle beam weapon will probably not be deployed before the twenty-first century, the technology holds such promise that the Strategic Defense Initiative Organization funded a dedicated particle beam test bed at the Brookhaven National Laboratory. SDI planners seem confident that neutral particle beams have practical applications for both sensor and weapons missions in the strategic defense system.

Patriot

System type: Ground-based missile interceptor
Country of origin: USA
Manufacturer: Raytheon
Principal distinguishing feature: As of 1991, the only battle-tested, anti-ballistic missile system in the field
Status: Production

Raytheon's Patriot air defense system went to Saudi Arabia in 1990 as a promising new weapon and came back a household world. During Operation *Desert Storm* in January-February 1991, Patriot missiles successfully downed numerous Iraqi Al-Abbas and Al-Hussein (NATO codename Scud) Intermediate Range Ballistic Missiles (IRBMs).

Secretary of Defense Richard Cheney said after the war that 'If we have learned anything from Scud missiles, it is how a country could be held hostage to even an old weapon without a proper defense.' The Patriot had provided the proper defense.

As Lawrence Korb of the Brookings Institute said at the time, 'The Patriot is an amazing story. Everyone seems surprised because it is doing what it is supposed to do.'

During Operation *Hammer* training exercises in Europe in 1986, 1987 and 1988, Patriots had achieved an outstanding performance, and in 1987 the US Army issued a multi-year contract calling for delivery of 6077 missiles and 104 fire control units. By the time of Operation *Desert Storm*, the US Army had deployed 10 Patriot battalions worldwide. The Army deployed Patriot to the 32d Air Defense Command in Europe and the 11th Air Defense Brigade in the United States. The 32d is integrated into the NATO Air Defense force structure, and the 11th Air Defense Brigade's assets support worldwide contingency operations, such as Operation *Desert Storm*.

In test programs, the Patriot demonstrated capability to counter the aircraft threat, including saturation raids, high speed targets, highly maneuverable targets and in sophisticated electronic counter measures (ECM) environments. Patriot fire power, in terms of rapid rate of fire, fast reaction time and multiple, simultaneous engagements meets, or exceeds, all specified requirements.

Looking to the twenty-first century, the Patriot will be the cornerstone of both the US Army European and Contingency Forces' integrated air defense system. The Patriot system is effective against very advanced ECM threats, and the enhanced system survivability resulting from inherent Patriot mobility is very impressive. As Representative Charles E Bennett of Florida said in 1991, 'We can all be proud of the Patriot system. It is the kind of practical, workable antimissile system we should be producing.'

RAH-66 Comanche

System type: Light attack/reconnaissance helicopter
Country of origin: USA
Manufacturer: Boeing and Sikorsky
Principal distinguishing feature: The first helicopter to incorporate stealth technology
Status: Selected for US Army service by the end of the twentieth century, and under consideration elsewhere

The US Army's LH Program was conducted during the late 1980s and directed at developing a light, fast and versatile attack and reconnaissance helicopter to equip 23 divisions by the year 2000. The LH would be the first known helicopter designed to incorporate the sort of stealth characteristics that had first appeared a decade earlier in fixed-wing aircraft. Two contractor teams were selected to submit proposals: Bell/McDonnell Douglas and Boeing/Sikorsky. This

was curious because at the same time Bell and Boeing were teamed up to build the V-22 Osprey.

In April 1991, the Boeing/Sikorsky team was selected to build the LH under the designation RAH-66 (Reconnaissance/Attack, Helicopter type, 66th). The name Comanche was chosen because names of Indian tribes are always assigned to US Army helicopters and because, in the Army's words, the Comanche were 'superior scouts and fierce fighters,' characteristics expected of the RAH-66.

Powered by an Allison-Garrett T800 engine, the RAH-66 could fly at 200 mph and execute a 90-degree turn at 100 mph in 5.5 seconds. It had a very low radar cross-section and a rate of climb of 1182 feet per minute, more than double the Army's requirement. It is equipped with the Longbow Radar,

first tested on the AH-64 Apache, and could carry out autonomous attacks against enemy positions that were heavily defended electronically, (such as the Iraqi air defenses, which were attacked on 17 January 1991 by AH-64s), but only with the support of CH-53 Pave Low helicopters.

The RAH-66 is very versatile. It can be disassembled and loaded into a C-130 or C-17 airlifter in 20 minutes and reassembled in 22 minutes. The US Army intends to spend $2.8 billion to buy 1292 through 2010, and the United Kingdom has considered the Comanche to replace the Westland Lynx after 2005.

Below, left: A full-scale mock-up of the Boeing Sikorsky Comanche helicopter is pictured with missile bays open and 20mm cannon deployed. *Below, right:* Sporting desert colors, the Comanche quickly converts from its stealthy scout role into an attack helicopter.

Center: J Duncan Smith's cutaway of the RAH-66 Comanche. Note the way that the main rotor shaft and engines are fully enclosed, unlike earlier helicopters. This surface blending helps the RAH-66 to reduce the RAH-66's radar cross section. Also note the RAH-66's retractable landing gear.

Rafale

System type: Fifth generation fighter aircraft
Country of origin: France
Manufacturer: Dassault-Breguet
Principal distinguishing feature: A very fast and versatile fifth generation aircraft
Status: Operational status achieved in mid-1990s in France and probably in several export markets by 2000

The Dassault-Breguet Mirage 2000, which entered service in 1983, was seen as the optimum French fighter for the turn of the century. The Rafale (hailstorm) is seen as the backbone of the French air force (*Armée de l'Air*) in the years *after* 2000. The Rafale is a fast, lightweight fighter with a high degree of maneuverability achieved through the use of canard control surfaces similar to those of the British Aerospace EAP, which was developed simultaneously in the United Kingdom. Like all of the latest generation jet fighters, it incorporates digital fly-by-wire avionics and is constructed with a high percentage of carbon fiber composite material. Armament centers on a 30mm DEFA-554 cannon and wingtip mounted Matra Magic air-to-air missiles.

France would also like to see the Rafale as an export product and, indeed, Dassault-Breguet, France's premier warplane builder for nearly four decades, has a customer base in as many as 26 countries. Dassault-Breguet has in fact proposed the Rafale to NATO nations as a successor to the General Dynamics F-16 or as an alternative to the Eurofighter EFA, and Saudi Arabia has expressed a great deal of interest as well. France itself is tentatively planning for 250 Rafales for its air force and 85 for its navy.

Built at St Cloud, the Rafale A prototype was shipped to Dassault-Breguet's test field at Istres in December 1985, from which it made its first flight on 4 July 1986. Guy Mitaux-Maurouard, Dassault-Breguet's chief test pilot, took the Rafale up to Mach 1.3 and 36,000 feet on this first flight.

The Rafale A was powered by a General Electric F404 turbofan engine, but the production Rafale Ds will all be equipped with French-built Snecma M88 turbofans. Approval for development of the Rafale D came in April 1988, and in October 1988, after test operations from the carrier *Foch*, the French navy decided to go ahead with its development of a carrier-based Rafale M (Marine) to replace the Vought F-8Es then in service.

The first Rafale C preproduction aircraft—essentially identical to the Rafale D—was delivered in 1991. It was 50 feet, three inches long, compared to 51 feet, 10 inches for the Rafale, and had a wingspan of 35 feet, 10 inches, compared to 36 feet. Equipped with the Snecma M88, it first flew on 19 May 1991, exceeding Mach 1.2 and reaching 36,000 feet. The Mirage 200 chase plane couldn't keep up—even with its afterburner!

By the twenty-first century, the Rafale will be the standard tactical aircraft of the France and perhaps of the air forces of many other European countries.

These pages: The Rafale, France's fifth generation fighter aircraft, is the latest nationally-produced French advanced technology fighter. Dassault-Breguet has proposed the Rafale to NATO nations as a successor to the General Dynamics F-16 and the EFA. Developed at the same time as the Eurofighter consortium's EFA, the Rafale will be the backbone of the French air force into the twenty-first century.

Rail Gun Systems

System type: ICBM Interceptors
Country of origin: USA/Former USSR
Manufacturer: Various
Principal distinguishing feature: These systems use hypervelocity projectiles to destroy ICBMs or other targets
Status: Experimental

Rail guns utilize a system of electromagnets to launch projectiles. These guns would have very high muzzle velocities, thereby reducing the lead angle required to shoot down fast-moving objects. If fired in the atmosphere, this fast muzzle velocity would flatten trajectories.

Hypervelocity rail guns are, at least conceptually, an attractive alternative for a space-based defense system. This is because of their envisioned ability to quickly 'shoot' at many targets. Also, because only the projectile leaves the gun, the gun can carry many projectiles.

A hypervelocity rail gun works very much like a nuclear accelerator. A metal pellet (the projectile) is attracted down a guide (the rail) of magnetic fields and accelerated by the rapid on-off switching of the various fields. The speeds attained by these small projectiles are dazzling. In one experiment a small particle was accelerated to a velocity of more than 24 miles per second. (At that speed, the projectile could circle the earth at the equator in something less than 20 minutes.)

The Compact High Energy Capacitor Module Advanced Technology Experiment (CHECMATE), managed by the Strategic Defense Initiative Office (SDIO) of the Defense Department, was to fire two projectiles per day as early as the mid-1980s. This represents a significant improvement over previous efforts, which were only able to achieve about one shot per month.

In the 1960s, the Soviet Union developed an experimental gun that could shoot streams of particles of heavy metals, such as tungsten or molybdenum, at speeds of nearly 15 miles per second in air and over 36 miles per second in a vacuum. The former Soviet Union also has a variety of ongoing research programs in the area of kinetic energy weapons. Such weapons destroy targets through the use of nonexplosive projectiles moving at very high speeds. The projectiles may include homing sensors and onboard rockets to improve accuracy, or they may follow a pre-set trajectory, much like a shell launched from a gun or cannon. The projectile could be launched from a rocket, a conventional gun or a rail gun.

One of the major technical challenges of the rail gun system is the rapid firing of the gun. The challenge has to do with the rails. In order to rapidly accelerate the pellet, the rail must rapidly switch its magnetic fields on and off. This extremely fast switching requires a tremendous current of

Below: The experimental USAF Sagittar, as shown in this artist's concept, is a space-based electromagnetic rail gun designed to intercept ICBMs or destroy targets.

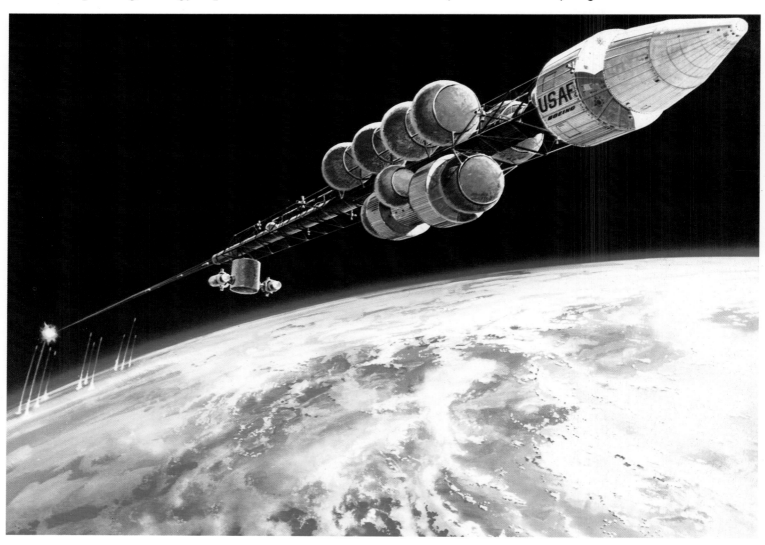

electricity (almost one-half million amperes) to pass through the rails every time the gun is fired. In some experiments, the rails had to be replaced after each firing.

Another challenge with the rail gun is the rapid acceleration of the projectile. At the speeds mentioned above, the acceleration stresses the pellet to pressures in excess of 100,000 times the normal force of gravity. In more popular terms, the acceleration of the pellet can be expressed in terms of 100,000 'Gs.' A 'G' is the acceleration of an object which is acted upon by gravity. If we drop a rock from a bridge, for instance, that rock will pick up speed at the rate of one G. As a passenger of a modern jetliner, you are pushed into your seat at takeoff by the one to two G acceleration. Imagine the six to nine Gs felt by fighter pilots in today's performance aircraft. On the average, humans tend to black out at about 10 Gs.

Even with this limited view of G forces, it is easy to understand that the jolt of explosive acceleration in a rail gun could easily tear the bullet apart. In order to be effective, the bullet must be able to withstand the initial acceleration in order to get to the target. Further, if there ever were to be homing devices in larger rail gun projectiles, that projectile would need to be hardened to keep its shape, and the electronics inside it would need to be able to function after being stressed by the initial acceleration.

At the approach of the millennium, rail guns were still only a step this side of science fiction, but in the twenty-first century, they will represent an integral part of any high-technology arsenal.

Rooikat

System type: Wheeled, armored fighting vehicle
Country of origin: South Africa
Manufacturer: Armscor
Principal distinguishing feature: A highly mobile, Third World developed, armored vehicle
Status: Production

It has now been documented that the role of Armored Fighting Vehicles in operations around the world is being re-examined with the advent of a new generation of fast, highly mobile, wheeled Armored Fighting Vehicles (AFVs). Clearly, wheeled AFVs can never fully replace main battle tanks in conventional warfare, as the tanks have the advantage of heavier armor and the increased fire power of their larger main guns. However, the upgraded development of what used to be known as an armored reconnaissance vehicle, coupled with evolving techniques in high mobility warfare, is causing military strategists to entirely rethink the battlefields of today—and the twenty-first century.

As the United States discovered in Vietnam, the tank's perceived advantages actually become handicaps when

Below: The Rooikat has been specifically designed for 'high-mobility warfare.' High speed and superior fire power make it ideally suited to the role of a hunter/killer.

translated into low mobility, vulnerability, heavy maintenance and high operating costs. These considerations eventually led to the emergence of wheeled armored vehicles which, as a result of recent advances in automotive technology, weaponry, fire control systems and cost effectiveness, now enjoy the status of full-fledged combat vehicles. The development of high-velocity, armor-piercing, fin-stabilized, discarding-sabot ammunition now provides relatively small caliber guns with the capability to destroy modern main battle tanks.

A major part of the idea behind the Rooikat was the South African desire to develop a strong, indigenous capability to design and produce advanced weapons systems. As such, South Africa's case is prototypical of the kind of industries that will emerge in the twenty-first century around the world in countries which have in the past depended on North America and Europe for high technology weaponry.

The Rooikat was originally developed to fulfill South Africa's combat reconnaissance needs during high-mobility operations, such as seek-and-destroy missions deep into enemy territory. For this reason, it has been designed to engage and destroy a wide variety of targets over all types of terrain and in all kinds of weather.

In the development of the Rooikat, the designers selected the concept of a wheeled vehicle. Overall, the weapons system is a unique balance of mobility, fire power and protection which make it optimally suited to its role. An operating range of 600 miles and a top speed of 80 mph afford the Rooikat exceptional strategic mobility. Cross-country speeds of up to 40 mph, good acceleration and obstacle-crossing capabilities ensure high tactical agility.

The Rooikat has a 76mm gun which fires specially developed, armor-piercing (APFSDS/T) rounds and standard high explosive (HE/T) rounds. The stabilized turret and integrated fire control system provide accuracy and low reaction time against tanks at ranges in excess of 750 feet and against soft-skinned targets at ranges of up to seven miles. A high level of protection is provided against enemy projectiles, land mines and chemical attacks. Even with two wheels destroyed on the same side, the vehicle can still reach a safe area. A high level of user friendliness has been attained, which greatly enhances crew alertness and efficiency.

Among the various Armored Fighting Vehicles in production (or under development) around the world, the Rooikat is typical of a new generation of vehicles that face unpredictable tests in the twenty-first century.

Sänger/CARGUS

System type: Two-stage spaceplane
Country of origin: Germany
Manufacturer: Deutsch Aerospace (incorporating Messerschmitt Bölkow Blohm)
Principal distinguishing feature: Likely to be the most advanced horizontal takeoff spaceplane in service in the early twenty-first century
Status: Development, with flight status to be achieved soon after 2000

In Germany during World War II, Dr Eugen Sänger (1903-1964) designed a horizontally launched, two-stage orbital spaceplane that he envisioned as being used as a bomber to strike targets in the United States or anywhere in the world. Sänger's revolutionary craft was never produced, but it did inspire a great many spaceplane design efforts in the 1950s, which culminated in the Boeing X-20 in the 1960s. In the 1980s the German government decided to undertake development of a spaceplane based on Sänger's original concept, which would be named for him. The project would be sponsored by the German Ministry for Research and Technology (BMFT) and the German Aerospace Research Agency (DLR), with participation by other members of the European Space Agency (ESA) as well.

Unveiled in August 1986, the Sänger vehicle is seen by the Germans as a successor to the French Hermes spaceplane in the context of ESA-supported manned space flight. The principal contractors for the project—all in Germany—will be Messerschmitt-Bölkow-Blohm (MBB) for aerodynamics, guidance and navigation and Dornier for materials and structures. The engines will be constructed by Motoren & Turbinen Union (MTU).

First exhibited at the Paris Air Show in June 1989, the Sänger was suggested to be a horizontally-launched, completely reusable craft consisting of two stages, each of which would be aerodynamic spaceplanes. The larger of these, the first stage, would be 275 feet long, with a gross weight of 700,000 pounds, making it the same size as the largest jetliners. The second stage would consist of either the

Below: A 1:8.5 scale model of the Sänger reusable, two-stage aerospace plane during its 1991 rollout.

manned Hypersonic Orbital Upper Stage (HORUS) or the unmanned Cargo Upper Stage (CARGUS). The huge SCRAMJET (Supersonic Combustion Ramjet) powered first stage would carry the second stage to Mach 6.8 and an altitude of 19 miles, where it would be released to fly into space under its own rocket propulsion.

Both HORUS and CARGUS would be over 100 feet long and would be in the same size and weight class as the American Space Shuttle and Soviet Kosmolyet orbiters, although plans are under consideration to scale them down because the payload capacity is not needed.

The Sänger project is similar to the American X-30 and French *Avion à Grande Vitesse* (AGV) single-stage-to-orbit aircraft, insofar as all are designed for horizontal takeoffs and are capable of carrying payloads roughly equal to those now carried by the Soviet and American shuttle systems.

A precursor to Sänger may be the horizontal takeoff, Mach

Above: Illustrator Erik Viktor rendered this view of the Sänger space transportation system at an altitude of about 20 miles.

5.5 Hypersonic Technology Experimental vehicle (HYTEX) which MBB unveiled in November 1990. HYTEX would weigh 44,100 pounds and would be 75 feet long, with a wingspan of 30 feet. It would be powered by four turbo ramjets burning kerosene in their turbo mode and liquid hydrogen as they reached the Mach 5 environment under ramjet power. Test flights would take place at 91,900 feet, either over the Atlantic Ocean off Portugal, over the North Sea off Denmark or between Sicily and Sardinia over the Mediterranean.

It is indeed a fitting tribute to the man who conceived winged, horizontal takeoff spacecraft in the mid-twentieth century that one such vehicle bearing his name will take wing in the twenty-first century.

SDIO SSTO

System type: Single-stage-to-orbit manned spacecraft
Country of origin: USA
Manufacturer: Boeing, General Dynamics, McDonnell Douglas or Rockwell International
Principal distinguishing feature: SSTO technology is, in itself, a distinguishing feature, but this system involves a very tight deployment schedule
Status: Initial contract issued in 1990, with operational status to be achieved by 1997

In November 1990, as work on the X-30 NASP project was proceeding, the SDIO announced that it would like to build its *own* Single-Stage-to-Orbit (SSTO) vehicle. 'We believe the technology for a rocket-powered SSTO is here today,' said Lt Col Pat Ladner, USAF, who became the SDIO's SSTO program director. The mission of such a vehicle would include delivery into orbit of Brilliant Pebbles interceptors, as well as supporting space stations and maintaining two astronauts for a four-day mission.

A series of contracts, averaging between $2.4 and $3 million, were issued to Boeing, General Dynamics, McDonnell Douglas and Rockwell International. The project called for a craft with a gross weight of 1.2 million pounds and a payload of 20,000 pounds. SDIO envisioned demonstration flights around 1994, and a operational flight by 1997, insisting that this SSTO was a real vehicle and not a 'paper program.'

Above: An artist's concept of the SSTO vehicle being developed for the SDIO. Known as the 'Delta Clipper,' the vehicle would deliver spaced-based weapons systems into orbit.

Su-27

System type: Fourth generation fighter aircraft
Country of origin: former USSR
Manufacturer: Sukhoi OKB
Principal distinguishing feature: The most advanced Soviet combat aircraft prior to the 1991 Revolution and the first non-V/STOL aircraft to fly from a Soviet aircraft carrier
Status: Operational status achieved by late 1980s is expected to continue well into the twenty-first century

In 1986, the Soviet Air Force took delivery of the Su-27 (NATO codename Flanker), which was then the best and most advanced fighter ever produced by the Sukhoi OKB, and perhaps in the Soviet Union. Like the MiG-29, the Su-27 is a twin-tailed, twin-engined jet fighter that employs blended contour construction which utilizes carbon fiber components. It is also endowed with pulse-Doppler look-down/shoot-down radar like that of the MiG-29.

First tested in 1977, the Su-27 is now built at Komsomolsk near Khabarovsk. The Su-27 is in the same size and weight

Above: The Su-27 serves as interceptor and long-range escort.

class as the McDonnell Douglas F-15 and probably owes something of its design inspiration to the F-15. In service since 1986, the Su-27 was first seen in the West when a pair of them were displayed at the Paris Air Show in June 1989. The Su-27's aerobatic demonstration was as impressive as the debut of the MiG-29 a year earlier at Farnborough, England, and it also included the thrilling tail slide maneuver.

A twin-engined fighter with a positive thrust-to-weight ratio, the Su-27 is powered by a pair of Lyulka AL-31 turbofans delivering 27,500 pounds of thrust. A specially enhanced Su-27, known internally as P-42, was used to achieve four major time-to-height records, including a climb to 39,370 feet in 55.5 seconds.

The Su-27 is a single-seat aircraft, although a small number of nearly identical, combat capable, dual seat Su-27U (*Uti*) training variants have also been produced.

Like the MiG-29, the Su-27 is armed with a 30mm cannon. Its additional armament consists of seven to ten air-to-air missiles, including AA-8, AA-10 and AA-11 types. Provisions for air-to-ground armament are also present, but this is a decidedly secondary role.

Roughly 100 Su-27s were delivered in the first three years

of service, with these being assigned principally to the Legnica and Vinnitsa air armies of the Soviet air force. Ultimately, they will be used both as interceptors and as long-range escorts for the Su-24. With their long range, both the Su-24 and Su-27 have the capability of reaching targets throughout Western Europe (including Britain) from Warsaw Pact bases. In the interceptor role, the Su-27's look-down/shoot-down radar makes it very effective against low-flying aircraft and cruise missiles.

The Su-27 was also used by the Soviet navy aboard its first full-size aircraft carrier, the *Tbilisi*, which began qualification trials in 1989 and became operational in 1991. With the collapse of the USSR in December 1991, the Su-27 automatically became a key player in the arsenals of the formerly constituent republics. With this in mind, it is expected to become one of the primary fighter aircraft in the navies and air forces of these republics in the 1990s, and to remain in this role well into the next century.

Timberwind

System type: Nuclear-powered, space-launch vehicle
Country of origin: USA
Manufacturer: TBA
Principal distinguishing feature: Potentially the most powerful space-launch vehicle ever deployed
Status: Highly classified SDIO/USAF study

During the 1960s, the United States studied numerous ways of using nuclear propulsion for space travel, notably the joint NASA/Atomic Energy Commission project known

as Nuclear Engine for Rocket Vehicle Application (NERVA). The NERVA project was intended to develop the engine for NASA's famous 1981 manned expedition to Mars, preparation for which was canceled in 1969. After extensive and somewhat promising experiments had been conducted at a Nevada test site, NERVA itself was canceled in 1972. The concept resurfaced more than 10 years later as Project Timberwind. Babcock & Wilcox built a subscale reactor for the Brookhaven National Laboratory about 1985 under Project Pipe, and this seems to be the basis for Timberwind, a 'black' SDI project not known outside SDIO until April 1991.

Timberwind involves Nuclear Thermal Rockets (NTRs) in which rocket fuel, such as hydrogen, flows through a reactor and is heated before flowing through the nozzle. Although the heat is no greater than a typical hydrogen/oxygen chemical rocket, there would be a higher specific impulse because hydrogen has a lower molecular weight than hydrogen plus oxygen.

In the fall of 1990, concepts were delivered to SDIO outlining conversion of General Dynamics Atlas or Martin Marietta Titan launch vehicles to Timberwind test beds that would use eight NRVs, each with 250,000 pounds of thrust. This could put up to 70 tons of payload into low-earth orbit.

Initially, Timberwind was to be the SDIO's means of launching large numbers of Brilliant Pebbles interceptors. However, in July 1991, Stanley Browski at NASA's Nuclear Propulsion Systems Office told the International Conference on Emerging Nuclear Energy Systems that 'If you want

Below: The Titan IV's first launch in 1989. The Titan could form the basis for an operational Timberwind.

to initiate major lunar activity where significant amounts of cargo and people are sent to the moon routinely, Nuclear Thermal Rockets can do it more efficiently and cost effectively than chemical rockets.'

This was, as SDIO would have pointed out, certainly true of Earth orbit, but Browski added the tantalizing promise of Timberwind NRVs doing what NERVA NRVs might have done a decade earlier—send humans on a fast trip to the planet Mars. On 15 January 1992, the US Air Force Space Technology Test Center at Kirtland AFB, New Mexico, formally proposed using Timberwind as a system to make a six-month Mars mission a reality early in the twenty-first century.

TR-3 Black Manta

System type: Stealth reconnaissance aircraft
Country of origin: USA
Manufacturer: Northrop
Principal distinguishing feature: Triangular airframe stealth aircraft
Status: Operational within a top secret veil

Stories of mysterious, black flying wings go back to the 1960s, but the first studies leading to the TR-3 seem to date from 1976 and the Air to Surface Technology Evaluation & Integration (ASTEI) program. At least 10 stealth aircraft programs—including Have Blue, which led to the Lockheed F-117—were undertaken in this same time frame. ASTEI led to the Covert Survivable In-weather Reconnaissance/Strike (CSIRS) program, which in turn led to both the F-117 (the strike aircraft) and the TR-3 (the reconnaissance aircraft).

Northrop got a contract in late 1978 to build a Tactical High-Altitude Penetrator (THAP) prototype. This aircraft, the XTR-3 or YTR-3, first flew in 1981 at Groom Lake, Nevada, and led to the production of up to 30 TR-3As. These have in turn been observed often since 1989 between Nellis AFB, Nevada, and Edwards AFB, California, and White Sands, New Mexico. Occasionally, TR-3s were seen in the company of F-117s, and during Operation *Desert Storm* in 1991, TR-3s are reported to have flown reconnaissance missions over Iraq in support of F-117 combat operations. Probably powered by two General Electric F404 turbofans buried in its wings, the TR-3 is quieter than the F-117 and about the same size, being 42 feet long with a 65-foot wingspan.

Uzi Mini Submachine Gun

System type: 9mm, 600 rpm automatic infantry weapon
Country of origin: Israel
Manufacturer: Israel Military Industries (IMI)
Principal distinguishing feature: Lightweight, durable and versatile infantry weapon
Status: Production

In the world of light infantry weapons, the name Uzi has become synonymous with all-round reliability, and is likely to remain so in the twenty-first century. The basic Uzi is lightweight, air-cooled and magazine fed, and can be fired in either full automatic or semiautomatic mode, from the

Below: The 9mm Uzi mini submachine gun exemplifies the reliability and durability that the name Uzi has come to represent.

hip or shoulder. Three independent safety features make the Uzi among the safest of all automatic weapons. A thumb operated fire selector blocks the trigger when in 'safe' position. The grip safety, at the rear of the pistol grip, must be depressed before the weapon will fire, thus preventing accidental discharge. A retracting safety ratchet keeps the bolt from sliding forward and the weapon from firing, even if the operator's hand should slip off the cocking knob while cocking. Famous for its accuracy and safety, the Uzi is even more famous for its reliability. Battle proven in thousands of engagements in environments ranging from snow to desert, the Uzi's ability to keep firing in the presence of sand, dust and water has made it the standard against which other weapons are judged.

This weapon is designed for operation with equal ease by left or right-handed shooters. For greater versatility, 20-, 25- and 32-round magazines are standard and available. Stripping and cleaning are quick and easy, and maintenance is simple. Only five parts are involved in stripping the Uzi, and the entire operation is routinely accomplished without tools in 10 seconds. A complete inventory of spare parts is always available.

With metal stock, the Uzi weighs 125 ounces, and is 25.6 inches long with the stock extended; 18.5 inches long with the stock folded. Although the total length of the weapon is only 18.5 inches, the unique sleeved bolt of the Uzi allows it to accommodate a 10.25-inch barrel. This Uzi is rifled right hand, one turn in 10 inches.

Below: A 9mm carbine variant of the Uzi mini submachine gun.

Uzi Semiautomatic Carbine

System type: 9mm carbine variant of the mini submachine gun
Country of origin: Israel
Manufacturer: Israel Military Industries (IMI)
Principal distinguishing feature: Designed to be an all-weather, all-environment carbine
Status: Production

Like its predecessor, this weapon has a good reputation, which is likely to continue in the twenty-first century. The Uzi 9mm semiautomatic carbine will continue firing in rain, snow, sandstorms, desert heat or sub-zero weather. In addition to its safety catch, the Uzi carbine has a safety grip that has to be squeezed all the way, or the carbine won't fire. The Uzi carbine is pre-zeroed at the factory, and provides 2.9-inch groups at 109 yards. Adjustment of the rear sight for windage and the front sight for elevation (or individual eyesight) is simple; the optionally available sight adjustment tool does the job in seconds. Sight guards protect both sights against accidental knocks. The Uzi semiautomatic carbine weighs just 9.5 pounds, and is 31.5 inches long, with metal stock extended.

The carbine conversion kit allows one to fire .22 caliber long rifle ammunition without any modifications to the carbine itself. You will then be able to practice firing on enclosed ranges using inexpensive ammunition. The kit

includes the following main parts: .22 caliber carbine barrel; bolt housing/ striker assembly, including the bolt housing and ejector; and the magazine assembly—this is a carbine magazine housing, modified to take the special .22 caliber magazine.

V-22 Osprey

System type: Tilt-rotor tactical airlifter
Country of origin: USA
Manufacturer: Bell Helicopter Textron/Boeing Helicopter
Principal distinguishing feature: The first tilt-rotor aircraft designed to be an operational prototype
Status: Regardless of whether budget constraints kill or hamper the V-22 program, V-22 technology will certainly survive and/or resurface by the early twenty-first century

The Osprey evolved out of the XV-15 project and made its first flight powered by Allison T406 engines on 23 March 1989 at Arlington, Texas. The venture, based on an idea that dates back to the Vietnam War, undertaken jointly by Boeing Helicopter and Bell Helicopter Textron, was to build a practical aircraft that could take off vertically like a helicopter, fold its huge rotors down and then use them to fly like an airplane.

This concept seemed ideal for 'special operations' or commando raids where no runways were available and where a craft was needed that had greater lifting power and greater speed than a conventional transport helicopter. The V-22 could also be used to effect vertical take-offs and landings on virtually any type of ship. The US Marine Corps planned to buy 552, while the Air Force and Navy intended to procure 105 between them.

Within a month of the first flight, Defense Secretary Richard Cheney announced his decision to cancel the V-22 project for budgetary reason. Congress, however, kept the program alive by deciding to postpone a final cancellation decision. Despite Navy termination on 1 December 1989,

(continued on page 70)

Below: In numerous tests the Bell-Boeing V-22 has bested transport helicopters in lifting capability, speed and efficiency. In time, its tilt-rotor technology will become a reality.

These pages: The versatile Bell-Boeing V-22 Osprey demon-strates the vertical take-offs and landings that would, and indeed should, make it a prime candidate for commando missions and which enable it to land on virtually any type of ship.

Above: A prototype V-22 Osprey in USMC camouflage colors.

(continued from page 67)

Congress continued to fund the program and six aircraft. No 1 would be used to test the flight envelope. No 2 would be used by Boeing to test primary and automatic flight control systems. No 3 would be used by Bell for flight load test and at-sea shipboard trials. No 4 would be used by Boeing for climatic tests at Eglin AFB. No 5 would be used for avionics and autopilot testing. No 6 would be used for radiation testing and operational evaluation.

The first conversion from the helicopter-like hover mode to full forward flight came on 14 September 1989. Shipboard tests were delayed until 4 to 7 December 1990, when No 3 and No 4 conducted a series of shuttle flights between the Naval Air Test Center at Patuxent River, Maryland and the helicopter attack carrier USS *Wasp* (LHD-1) offshore.

During early 1990, a study showed that a force of 105 V-22s and 28 CH-53 heavy lift helicopters could deliver twice as much firepower and airlift capacity as a force using 75 CH-53s and 88 H-60 utility helicopters. At the same time, Bell was talking to the Port Authority of New York and New Jersey about a fleet of 16-passenger Ospreys to fly between Newark Airport and midtown Manhattan. In Europe, a consortium called Eurfar introduced a model of an Osprey-like commercial tilt rotor at the Farnborough Air Show in September 1990. Still unimpressed, Secretary Cheney said in July 1990 that the Osprey wasn't worth the money, that it couldn't outperform helicopters well enough to make it worth the investment, despite its having won the 1990 Collier trophy! After Osprey No 5 suffered uncontrollable oscillation and crashed on its maiden flight on 11 June 1991, flight testing was put on an indefinite hold.

The V-22, or aircraft like it, will certainly be part of the world of combat aircraft. If the V-22 itself doesn't eventually go into production, it will form the basis for another which will. The idea is too good. If Congress doesn't buy it from Bell/Boeing, someone, somewhere will do it, and planes like these will be a reality in the twenty-first century.

The Walther WA 2000 with telescopic sight (left elevation).

Walther WA 2000

System type: Long-range precision rifle
Country of origin: Germany
Manufacturer: Walther Arms Works
Principal distinguishing feature: An infantry weapon exhibiting a high level of accuracy
Status: Production

By the time Germany's oldest major armsmaker celebrates its 150th anniversary in 2036, the Walther WA 2000 will have set a standard for its class. Accuracy, high performance ammunition, automatic function and gas operation were the main criteria specified during the development of the Walther Model WA 2000, designed around a high performance cartridge in order to achieve minimal impact variation. In comparative trials, the 300 Winchester Magnum provided the best results and was subsequently selected as the most suitable cartridge.

A highly accurate semiautomatic weapon, the target rifle Model WA 2000 is available in .300 Winchester Magnum. The .308 Winchester chambering is also available as an option.

All precision rifles available as late as the 1980s were derivatives of hunting or military weapons and, as such, invariably represented a compromise solution for the elite marksman who requires the ultimate in accuracy. The WA 200 was specially designed and built, and in combination with the .300 Winchester Magnum cartridge, it can be considered as weapon system offering optimal performance.

The primary structure of the weapon is a framework made of profiled tubing. The rear of this framework is firmly secured to the receiver, which accepts the bolt and the barrel. Ahead of the receiver in the vicinity of the telescopic sight mounting, the framework is reinforced by intermediate plates installed on both sides. The muzzle end of the profiled tubing is stiffened by a special construction.

The reason for this design was to create a self-supporting element in which the barrel would be symmetrically retained, and the recoil generated by the shot would be transmitted along the bore axis to the shooter's shoulder.

With this construction, there is no twisting movement, and the weapon remains on target. Consequently, no time is lost through target reacquisition. Trigger mechanism, striking device, trigger, trigger guard and safety are installed in the lower rail and form one unit. As the most important part of the weapon, the barrel is the deciding factor for accuracy. Consequently, internal and external design is critical. Groove and land diameters, twist and chambering are carefully matched to the caliber and are held within close tolerances. A muzzle brake is attached to the muzzle.

The weapon is gas operated. Its bolt head has seven locking lugs and rotates through 60 degrees. Gas tapped from a port in the barrel actuates a piston which initiates the unlocking cycle. The bolt stays open after the last shot. When the catch lever is thumbed down, the bolt runs forward and chambers a cartridge.

The weapon has a detachable, single-row magazine. Cartridge feed is arranged so that the bullet tip is not damaged during chambering. This is achieved by two cams on the follower plate, which also prevents the cartridge from slipping forward. The safety, which acts on the trigger and the sear, can be operated from both sides of the weapon.

This firearm can also be equipped with an adjustable bipod. Telescopic sights feature rapid adjustment for ranges from 328 to 984 feet and from 328 to 1640 feet, and can be supplied in the calibers .300 Winchester magnum and .308 Winchester. The rapid adjustment settings are calibrated with match ammunition to the respective optimal load combinations.

The scope mounts slide along a dovetail up to the forward stop and are retained by a clamping system. This makes sure that there is no wear on the mounts, as actual retention only takes place when the clamping force is applied. A spacer block is supplied with each weapon to provide optimal eye relief for the shooter.

Unlike conventional weapons which have plastic or wooden stocks, the WA 2000's frame is designed to accept the other parts. All these parts are attached independently to provide individual stock layout and final adjustment.

WIG see *Ekranoplan*

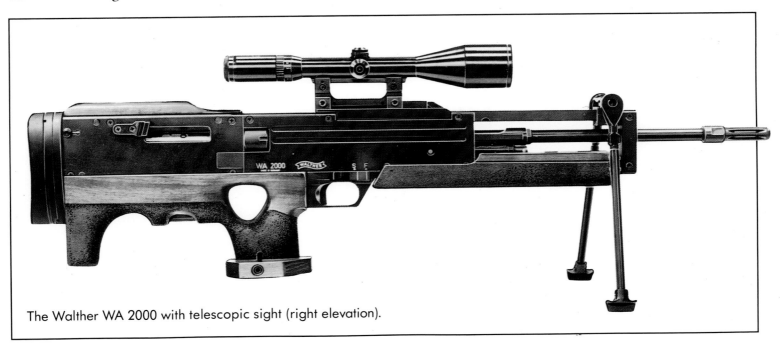

The Walther WA 2000 with telescopic sight (right elevation).

X-29

System type: Fighter aircraft demonstrator
Country of origin: USA
Manufacturer: Grumman
Principal distinguishing feature: Forward-swept wings to achieve unprecedented maneuverability
Status: Successful flight test program will lead to application of X-29 technology to other, more advanced, programs

The then radical notion of swept wings was first adopted in the 1940s, and that was soon determined to be the optimal configuration for jet aircraft flying at speeds of Mach .7 or greater. The idea of *forward*-swept wings evolved at the same time, and indeed the German Junkers Ju-287 jet bomber was flown with forward-swept wings in 1944. Theoretically, forward-swept wings provide more maneuverability at slower speeds than conventionally swept wings. However, the advantages seemed to be greatly outweighed by the problem of control. For this reason, forward-swept wings were used on smaller aircraft such as the postwar German Hansa Jet, but not seriously considered for high performance military aircraft until the 1970s, when high speed computers and digital fly-by-wire controls obviated the drawbacks.

The X-29 program began in 1977, sponsored by the US Defense Advance Research Projects Agency (DARPA), with Grumman being selected as the primary contractor in 1981. Two prototypes were built, the first being completed in 1984 and delivered to Edwards AFB for its first flight on 14 December 1984, with Grumman test pilot Chuck Sewell at the controls. The X-29 proved to be so maneuverable that

Sewell conducted a series of unauthorized barrel rolls on his third flight without any loss of control.

The first X-29 was flown for 242 flights, more than any of the other X-series aircraft, including the famous X-15, of which three individual aircraft made 199 flights between 1959 and 1968. During the course of these flights, test pilots from the US Air Force, US Navy and NASA took turns at the controls, evaluating forward-sweep technology, not only as a research project, but also from the standpoint of operational applications. The second X-29 arrived at Edwards AFB shortly before the first X-29 was permanently retired, and made its first flight on 23 May 1989. The test flight program, which took the X-29 to speeds of up to Mach 1.8, focused principally on maneuverability, especially high angle of attack maneuvering.

In the spring of 1992, the X-29 began to undergo a forward fuselage vortex control program, which, combined with earlier high angle of attack (AOA) tests, paved the way for remarkable twenty-first century aircraft maneuvering capability. This led USAF test pilot Major Dana Purifoy to describe the X-29 as 'a formidable machine at high AOA. The ability to fly to, and slightly beyond, the normal control envelope sets the X-29 apart from other aircraft. The X-29 has a very wide AOA envelope. The X-29 is a very honest aircraft. It exhibits all the features that I think you'd want in any future fighter flying at high angles of attack.' In the twenty-first century, the forward-swept wing technology evaluated by the X-29 in the 1980s and 1990s will be commonplace, as designers strive for the high degree of maneuverability that such a configuration permits.

Below: The X-29 made its second flight on 4 February 1985.

X-30 NASP

System type: Single-stage-to-orbit (SSTO) spaceplane
Country of origin: USA
Manufacturer: General Dynamics, McDonnell Douglas or Rockwell International
Principal distinguishing feature: The first American single-stage-to-orbit (SSTO) spaceplane
Status: Hampered by budget constraints, the X-30 may not be the first SSTO vehicle, but the technology derived from the program will be the foundation for a generation of American spaceplanes in the twenty-first century

Engineers around the world have had the concept of a hypersonic 'single-stage-to-orbit' spaceplane on drawing boards for nearly half a century, but the enormous costs and technical problems inherent in such a project have served to *keep* it on the drawing boards. The project specifically designated X-30 began in 1986 when NASA and the Department of Defense issued $450 million worth of development contracts to Boeing, General Dynamics, Lockheed, McDonnell Douglas and Rockwell International.

The scope of the project had been defined by President Ronald Reagan in his February 1986 State of the Union address, when he referred to the commercial potential of a National Aerospace Plane (NASP) that could be flown from the United States to Tokyo in only a few hours. The commercial NASP which Reagan described in his speech as the *Orient Express* was not the X-30, however, but rather a second generation NASP, part of a *family* of single-stage-to-orbit spaceplanes which will become common sights in the twenty-first century. The X-30 is also distinct from the NASA High Speed Civil Transport (HSCT) being developed by Boeing and McDonnell Douglas for service as early as the first decade of the twenty-first century. In fact, since 1987 the Defense Department (specifically Air Force Systems Command) role in the X-30 project has evolved to a much higher degree than the NASA civilian role. All artist conceptions that were originally released showing the X-30 in jolly 'Air Force One' type markings were recalled in April 1987 at the behest of Congress, as the program became more of a secret military project.

Originally, the X-30 was to have had its first atmospheric flight test in 1993, and this projection held true until July 1988, when President George Bush's White House National Space Council agreed to a first flight postponement to 1997 or beyond. The thinking surrounding the project had by this time progressed to wanting to keep NASP a 'research project' rather than a 'prototype development effort.' Unless the delay means that the X-30 is preceded into space by a

Below: The Rockwell X-30 NASP concept is still evolving.

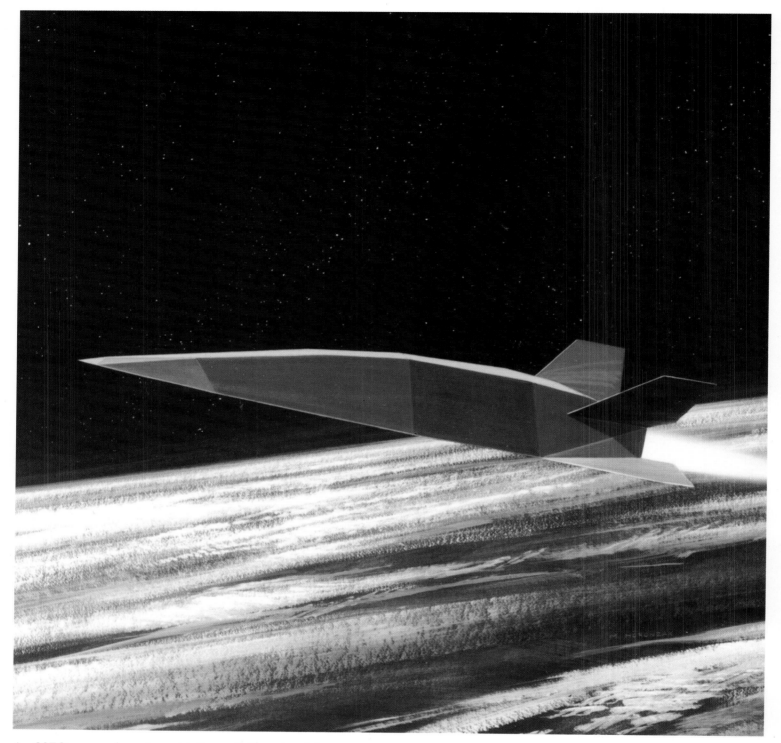

An SSTO spaceplane from McDonnell Douglas (above), and Rockwell's NASP (facing page).

German or international spaceplane, it will be the first craft capable of taking off from a runway, traveling into space and then landing on a runway at the end of its flight.

Delays have always, it seems, been chronic when engineers duel with politicians over schedules and funds. By October 1989, Vice President Dan Quayle (heading the National Space Council) and NASA administrator Richard Truly were increasingly ambivalent toward NASP, and funding was severely cut. By March 1991, however, the first design cycle had concluded, the range of configuration options had narrowed and a concrete picture of the X-30 had begun to emerge.

The X-30, of which probably two will be built, will have a titanium skeleton and will be approximately 150 feet long with a weight of 325,000 pounds, including about 100,000 pounds of fuel. The fuel being suggested is 'slush,' or partially frozen hydrogen, which is 16 percent more dense than liquid hydrogen and would offer a 30 percent savings in overall size and weight of the X-30. The use of five Scramjet (Supersonic Combustion ramjet) engines have also been proposed, but they are only practical between speeds of Mach 1 and Mach 6, and the X-30 will be operated between subsonic speeds and atmospheric re-entry speeds of Mach 25. Thus they will be augmented by two rocket engines—built by Rockwell Rocketdyne or Pratt & Whitney—with thrust in the range of 50,000 to 70,000 pounds. The fuel tanks may be an integral part of the structure, or they may be nonstructural elements made of graphite exoxy. Carbon

thermal panels will cover 25 percent of the surface, compared to the 85 percent of the Space Shuttle Orbiter's surface that is covered with tiles.

X-31

System type: Fighter aircraft demonstrator
Country of origin: Germany/USA
Manufacturer: Messerschmitt-Bölkow-Blohm/Rockwell International
Principal distinguishing feature: Vectorable-thrust engine to achieve unprecedented maneuverability
Status: Successful flight test program will lead to application of X-31 technology to other, more advanced, programs

The X-31 program was initiated to investigate and develop methods for achieving a high degree of maneuverability at high speed. The project dates back to 1981, when Rockwell International in California approached Messerschmitt-Bölkow-Blohm (MBB) in Germany, which at that time was working on preliminary designs for the European Fighter Aircraft (EFA). Rockwell had in mind a system for post-stall maneuvering at very low speeds through the use of canards and thrust vectoring. MBB liked the concept, but it was too late to include it in its EFA proposal.

Two years later, Rockwell approached the US Defense Advanced Research Projects Agency with a technology proposal it called 'Super-normal Kinetic Enhancement' (SNAKE). The essence of SNAKE was vectored engine thrust that was coordinated with aircraft control surfaces. SNAKE eventually evolved into Enhanced Fighter Maneuverability (EFM), which meant a regrettable loss of an acronym that perfectly described the way Rockwell's system would choreograph a flight.

In June 1986, the United States and Germany formalized an agreement to jointly sponsor development of a demonstration aircraft based on the EFM technology on which Rockwell and MBB had already been working for five years. The first of two X-31 aircraft was rolled out at Rockwell's Palmdale, California, test facility on 3 March 1990. The first flight took place on 11 October 1990, with Rockwell test pilot Ken Dyson at the controls. Three days later, he flew to 20,000 feet, achieving speeds up to Mach 0.6.

Within its first year of tests, the X-31 had already demonstrated an almost unparalleled capacity for maneuverability. While the new—and also very agile—Lockheed YF-22A prototype had done bank-to-bank turns at a 60 degree angle of attack, the X-31 had accomplished complete rolls at 70 degrees. The types of 'supermaneuver' of which the X-31 is capable are perhaps the ultimate in high performance fighter agility because of the G-force strain that such sudden and spectacular turns could potentially place upon the pilot. The EFM technology may well become standard equipment in the fighters of the twenty-first century, but to progress beyond this state-of-the-art will require advances not only in maneuvering technology but pilot survivability technology as well.

These pages: The X-31 drew from technology Rockwell and MBB had been developing for five years before a joint agreement to make EFM a reality cemented their partnership in 1986.

Above: This scene illustrated by Mark McCandlish shows X-31s outmaneuvering a pair of McDonnell Douglas F/A-18 Hornets. The F/A-18 is in the same size and weight class as the X-31 and serves primarily in the US Navy, the service which has shown the most interest in the production aircraft which will inevitably evolve from the X-31.

These pages: An artist's concept cutaway-view of the X-31 reveals the vectorable-thrust engine that is responsible for the enhanced maneuverability and is coordinated with aircraft control surfaces. The thrust-vectoring panels are clearly visible at the tail nozzle, aft of the General Electric F404 turbofan engine. The pink areas froward of the engine are the X-31's fuel tank. The F404 gives the X-31 a top speed in the Mach 1.3 range.

INDEX